MINUS SOME BUTTONS

a play in two acts

by

Mark Dunn

SAMUEL FRENCH, INC.

45 WEST 25TH STREET   NEW YORK 10010
7623 SUNSET BOULEVARD HOLLYWOOD 90046
LONDON   TORONTO

Copyright © 1991, 1991 by Mark Rodney Dunn

For Dorothy Gilliam

And Gordon Farrell

IMPORTANT BILLING AND CREDIT REQUIREMENTS

All producers of MINUS SOME BUTTONS *must* give credit to the Author of the Play in all programs distributed in connection with performances of the Play and in all instances in which the title of the Play appears for purposes of advertising, publicizing or otherwise exploiting the Play and/or a production. The name of the Author *must* also appear on a separate line, on which no other name appears, immediately following the title, and *must* appear in size of type not less than fifty percent the size of the title type.

Minus Some Buttons opened in New York City on October 11, 1990 at the Thirteenth Street Repertory Company. It was directed by Paul Michael. The set was designed by Mr. Michael. The dramaturg was Gordon Farrell. The lighting was by Emily Gadd. The costumes were designed by Patrick Lucey. The production stage manager was James Hughes III. The production technician was Rita Williams. The cast, in order of appearance, was as follows:

CLARENCE .... Michael Ben Kimmel
MYRTLE .... Jeanne Fleming
PENNY .... Rebecca VerNooy
RICHARD .... Kevin Brunnock
DORIS .... Sharon Shahinian
MS. DANLEY .... Marlene Hodgdon
JULES .... Jason Watt

CHARACTERS

CLARENCE OLANDER, mid to late forties—principal at Graceland Elementary School

MYRTLE DIXON, early to mid forties—Clarence's administrative assistant

PENNY PATTERSON, early thirties—the new fourth grade teacher at Graceland

RICHARD WINGFIELD, late twenties to early thirties—fourth grade teacher at Graceland

DORIS CRUMLEY, late twenties to early thirties—fourth grade teacher at Graceland

MS. DANLEY, thirties—Penny's own fourth grade teacher

JULES RICHTER, thirties—Superintendent of the Springdale City School System

(And the offstage voices of two children: Kevin and Beverly)

TIME AND PLACE

The play is set, for the most part, in the present, during early fall of this year, and covers a period of time from a few days before the first day of school to a few days after. Most of the action of the play takes place in Graceland Elementary School in the town of Springdale. In the writer's mind Springdale lies either in the south or the midwest ... or both, which, of course, means Oklahoma. Some of the scenes are set in the elementary school Penny attended as a child, and are conjured up through dream or memory.

Stage left is a classroom represented by a wooden teacher's desk and chair facing a small student desk. Behind the teacher's desk is a blackboard. Stage right are two office desks, each accompanied by two chairs—one for the occupant of the desk, the second set off to the side. There are telephones on each of these desks. On one sits a bust of Elvis Presley. On the other, a typewriter and self-standing public address microphone. Together these represent the inner and outer offices of Graceland Elementary School principal Clarence Olander. The desk with the microphone belongs to Clarence's administrative assistant, Myrtle. Near the classroom is a hallway; a door connecting the classroom to the hallway is implied. Its placement is left to the discretion of the director.

Note: The TSRC production did not hold to the illusion of separate offices for Clarence and Myrtle. In this production the principal and his assistant shared the same office, and a door to an outside hallway was placed upstage for use by them both. Also, the presence of various Elvis memorabilia cluttering these offices, while implied in the script, was quite in evidence in the set decoration used in the TSRC production.

ACT I

DAY ONE

In the darkness we hear a few bars of Elvis Presley singing "Blue Suede Shoes." MUSIC fades out as LIGHTS come up over Clarence and Myrtle's desks. CLARENCE sits at his desk, seemingly imprisoned behind a wall of paperwork. HE wears glasses, a summer jacket and a tightly knotted tie. Now and then HIS hand gropes for a bowl of pistachio nuts positioned in one corner of the desk. From time to time HE will pat his perspiring forehead with a handkerchief. MYRTLE, wearing a flowery summer blouse, shorts and sandals, enters the office and goes to her desk. SHE puts away her purse and straightens up a little.

CLARENCE. Is that *you*, Myrtle?

MYRTLE. (*Mischievously, her voice lowered an octave.*) No, it's the sunrise burglar. (*SHE smiles at her wit and waits for a response. When it doesn't come, SHE steps into Clarence's inner office and stares at him.*) Don't I even get a "Good morning"?

CLARENCE. (*Almost a mumble, without looking up.*) Good morning.

(CLARENCE continues to work. MYRTLE continues to stand and stare. HE finally looks up.)

CLARENCE. What's that?

MYRTLE. What?

CLARENCE. (*Pointing.*) The shorts.

MYRTLE. (*Modeling them.*) You like them?

CLARENCE. You know you're not supposed to come to work dressed like that.

MYRTLE. But I told you I was going to wear these shorts today.

CLARENCE. No you didn't.

MYRTLE. I most certainly did so. I said it right as I was walking out the door yesterday: "Goodbye, Clarence. Tomorrow I'm wearing shorts."

CLARENCE. I didn't hear you. Go home and change into a dress.

MYRTLE. I will not!

CLARENCE. I really don't have time for this right now.

MYRTLE. You know, Clarence, you've been such a grump since your prostate surgery.

CLARENCE. For God's sake, Myrtle!

MYRTLE. I realize that most of the fun went out of your life when Vivian died ...

CLARENCE. Can we please just—

MYRTLE. ... but lately it's like you're going for some kind of record or something.

CLARENCE. You could not have picked a worse time for this discussion, Myrtle.

MYRTLE. (*Responds by going to the empty chair by Clarence's desk and sitting down.*) I no longer look forward to coming to work in the morning.

CLARENCE. That makes two of us.

MYRTLE. I used to have such a good feeling about this school. Now I just don't know—

CLARENCE. Maybe it's the heat, Myrtle.

MYRTLE. Well, I'll agree the heat isn't helping things any. (*Mothering.*) Oh Clarence, look at you—sweating buckets under all those layers of clothes. At least take off the jacket.

CLARENCE. I'm all right.

MYRTLE. You look like one of those men in the sweat boxes—you know, where all you can see is their little wet bald heads poking out the top. (*SHE gets up to help Clarence out of his jacket.*) You would not believe what I saw on my way home from work yesterday. We were all lined up on the access ramp at Belmar—you know how the traffic always backs up during rush hour...

(*CLARENCE drapes the jacket over the back of his chair and sits back down.*)

MYRTLE. ... and these two men get right out of their trucks and start beating each other in the head with Playmate coolers.

CLARENCE. (*With minimal interest.*) That must have been a very odd sight.

MYRTLE. It was. (*Glancing out Clarence's window.*) I notice Mr. Yeager's truck out in the parking lot. Is he here this morning?

CLARENCE. Downstairs.

MYRTLE. Did he say if he'll have the air conditioning fixed by next week?

CLARENCE. I didn't ask. You can't communicate with Yeager when he's hungover like that. He throws tools at you.

MYRTLE. So are we assuming he *won't* have it fixed?

CLARENCE. I think that's wise. I'll put in a call to Richter and have him send over some fans for the classrooms.

MYRTLE. It would help if we could open the windows. You know, Clarence, I'd like to find the architect who designed this building and hang him up by his ... thumbs.

CLARENCE. We all would, Myrtle. But let's save that project for some day when we don't have so much work to do, okay?

(MYRTLE starts out.)

CLARENCE. Don't dawdle. Just change out of the shorts and come straight back.

MYRTLE. (*Whirling around angrily.*) No way, Clarence! I am *not* driving all the way home and put on something hot and uncomfortable just to satisfy your stupid dress code.

CLARENCE. (*Indicating Myrtle's outfit.*) I can't allow you to come to work wearing your backyard barbecue clothes. It gives the wrong impression.

MYRTLE. Who in Heaven's name are we giving the wrong impression to, Clarence? There's nobody here today but you and me and Mr. Yeager, and I'll bet you a chocolate sundae at Tastee Freeze, Yeager's wearing a hell of a lot less than I am right now.

CLARENCE. (*Overlapping.*) I asked—Myrtle, listen to me! I asked Ms. Patterson to come in this morning.

MYRTLE. Ms. Patterson—she's not that Elvis lady, is she?

CLARENCE. "Elvis lady?"

MYRTLE. You know—the woman who wants to buy all this ... (*Indicating various things around the office.*) ... Elvis stuff.

CLARENCE. No. You're thinking of Mrs. Pittman. That's *next* Friday. Ms. Patterson is the new fourth grade teacher—the one taking Angela's section.

MYRTLE. You're telling me I have to dress up for a *teacher?*

CLARENCE. (*Throwing up his hands.*) All right, Myrtle—you win. We'll forget about the dress code until after the air conditioning comes back on.

MYRTLE. You mean that? Clarence, you're a prince. (*SHE kisses him on the cheek.*)

CLARENCE. (*Squirming away.*) I'm not a prince. I'm just tired of discussing it. (*HE returns his attention to the work on his desk.*)

MYRTLE. I was going down to the teacher's lounge to get me a Pepsi. You want one?

CLARENCE. (*Without looking up.*) I don't drink sodas this early in the morning.

MYRTLE. (*Waggishly.*) All right then. I'll make you a nice hot cup of coffee.

CLARENCE. All right. All right. Get me a Pepsi. (*HE wipes his face with his handkerchief.*) I need to wash my face. (*HE gets up.*) Look, I'll get the sodas. You stay here and wait for Ms. Patterson.

(*HE starts out. MYRTLE follows him as far as her desk.*)

MYRTLE. If you run into Yeager in the hall, please make note of what he's wearing. If he's got on anything more than a tool belt, it'll be *my* treat.

CLARENCE. (*As HE goes.*) I'm sure it *will* be, Myrtle.

(SHE chuckles to herself, picks up a book from her desk and begins to fan her face. After a moment, PENNY enters. SHE is wearing a light summer skirt and blouse, and carries a large shoulder bag.)

PENNY. Good morning.

MYRTLE. Good morning.

PENNY. I'm here to see Mr. Olander.

MYRTLE. You must be Ms. Patterson.

PENNY. I am. (*As THEY shake hands.*) Although I prefer "Penny."

MYRTLE. And I prefer "Myrtle."

PENNY. You want to call me Myrtle?

MYRTLE. (*Laughs.*) Now that would be a little confusing, wouldn't it?

(PENNY laughs with her.)

MYRTLE. Mr. Olander has gone down the hall for a minute. Would you like something to drink?

(SHE gestures for Penny to sit down. THEY both sit.)

PENNY. I *am* a little parched—if it wouldn't be any trouble.

MYRTLE. No trouble at all. (*MYRTLE speaks into the p.a. microphone, her voice noticeably amplified.*) CLARENCE, ANOTHER DIET PEPSI PLEASE. PENNY PATTERSON JUST GOT HERE AND SHE'S AS THIRSTY AS SHE CAN BE. (*To Penny.*) You do look a little wilted.

PENNY. They haven't turned on the electricity in my apartment yet.

MYRTLE. (*Alarmed.*) You're not *staying* there, are you?

(*PENNY nods.*)

MYRTLE. How on earth are you managing that?

PENNY. I spend a lot of time in the bathtub. (*PENNY shows Myrtle her hands.*)

MYRTLE. Why, honey, you look like a wrinkly old woman. You shouldn't have to put yourself through this. There's a Motel 6 not two blocks from here.

PENNY. (*Starts to say something but nothing comes out. SHE touches her tongue.*) I'm sorry. For a moment I thought my tongue was glued to the roof of my mouth.

MYRTLE. Bless your heart. (*Into microphone.*) HURRY UP WITH THE SODAS, CLARENCE. MS. PATTERSON'S MOUTH IS AS DRY AS A BONE!

PENNY. I guess I'll never get used to these southern [midwestern] summers.

MYRTLE. Where are you from, honey?

PENNY. I grew up in Buffalo.

MYRTLE. I'd imagine the weather up there can get pretty extreme in the other direction.

PENNY. Oh yes.

MYRTLE. I read about people getting snowbound and having to eat their pet parakeets and things.

PENNY. I don't think it ever got that bad. I do remember a couple of very cold winters, though—back when I was a little girl. One year the heat went out in our school. The temperature must have dropped down to about twenty degrees inside. I remember sitting there in that icebox of a classroom, wondering if my toes were going to start falling off.

MYRTLE. That's horrible! (*Beat.*) How's your tongue?

PENNY. Better, thank you.

MYRTLE. (*Touching Penny's face.*) You look very flushed. You didn't walk here from your apartment, did you?

PENNY. (*Nodding.*) My car's in the shop. I lost my muffler on the drive down.

MYRTLE. Where do you live, honey?

PENNY. Sunny Meadows.

MYRTLE. That's an awfully long walk.

PENNY. I don't mind walking. When I was a little girl I used to walk five miles a day.

MYRTLE. There wasn't a school bus you could take?

PENNY. No, I don't mean walking to and from school. The walking we did was all right there on the playground. More like marching, really.

MYRTLE. Your teacher had you marching five miles a day?

PENNY. Six if we were especially naughty.

MYRTLE. I could just see Richard pulling a stunt like that.

PENNY. Who's Richard?

MYRTLE. Richard Wingfield. One of the other fourth grade teachers. Used to be a Marine drill sergeant. (*Confidentially.*) This should give you some idea about the kind of people you'll be working with here.

(*CLARENCE enters carrying three cans of soda.*)

MYRTLE. Clarence, this is Penny Patterson.
CLARENCE. (*Formally.*) Hello, Ms. Patterson.
PENNY. Hello.

(*CLARENCE fumbles a bit as HE attempts to shake hands with PENNY and give her a can of soda at the same time.*)

PENNY. Thank you.

(*CLARENCE gives one of the other two to MYRTLE.*)

CLARENCE. You're a little different from the way I pictured you during the phone interview.
PENNY. I am?
CLARENCE. I imagined you as looking older.
MYRTLE. (*To Penny.*) Show him your hands, honey. (*To Clarence.*) She has very old hands, Clarence.

(*PENNY and MYRTLE laugh. CLARENCE doesn't get it.*)

CLARENCE. Why don't we have a seat in my office?

(HE leads Penny into his private office. THEY both sit down. MYRTLE returns to her desk and will obviously be eavesdropping on the conversation which follows. PENNY looks about the room. CLARENCE offers her the pistachio nut bowl.)

CLARENCE. Nut?
PENNY. Who? (*Seeing the bowl.*) Oh, yes. Thank you.

(SHE takes a few of the nuts and will shell and eat them between sips from her can of soda. CLARENCE puts the nut bowl down and begins to search for something on his desk.)

PENNY. You have a very lovely office.
CLARENCE. Thank you.
PENNY. I've never seen so many pictures of Elvis Presley in one room.
CLARENCE. Yes, there do seem to be quite a few, don't there? (*HE finds what he's looking for: Penny's employment folder.*) Here we are.
PENNY. Are you a big fan of Elvis?
CLARENCE. I used to be. (*HE opens the folder.*) Oh— I should begin by apologizing for the heat.
PENNY. You don't have to apologize, Mr. Olander. Heat waves are an act of God.
CLARENCE. I was referring to the problem with the air conditioning.
PENNY. Well, I'm sure that's not your fault either. (*Indicating the soda.*) This really hits the spot.
CLARENCE. Glad you like it. Now—as I mentioned in my letter, I wanted to see you this morning for a couple

of reasons. As a rule I do like to visit with each of our new teachers before the start of the school year. This gives us a chance to get to know one another a little better, gives you the opportunity to ask me any questions you might have about the school or about specific school policies. Did you get the policy packet I sent you?

PENNY. Yes.

CLARENCE. And you've had a chance to look it over?

PENNY. Most of it. There are quite a few rules in there.

CLARENCE. This isn't a problem for you, is it?

PENNY. Oh no. Not at all.

CLARENCE. I didn't think it would be. Now—turning to your list of references. May I say how impressed I am with the names on this list? These are all highly respected educators.

PENNY. Yes, I know.

CLARENCE. Unfortunately, I didn't have the time to speak to even one of them. But that's what happens when you lose a teacher so suddenly as we did—not two weeks before the beginning of the new school year. You just aren't able to give the applicants as thorough a review as you would like.

PENNY. So, if you don't mind my asking—it was my references that gave me the edge over the others?

CLARENCE. Yes, along with that wonderful letter of recommendation from R.J. Covington. (*HE finds the letter.*) I think his endorsement alone would have convinced me that you were right for Graceland.

PENNY. So you're familiar with Mr. Covington's work?

CLARENCE. Quite. In fact, I can say in all honesty, I've probably read everything the man has ever published in the field of child management.

(PENNY seems happy to hear this.)

CLARENCE. I believe his book *Our Children, Our Wards* should be required reading for every education major in the country. (*Glancing at the letter in hand.*) You assisted with the research on that one?
PENNY. (*A little bashfully.*) Oh yes.
CLARENCE. Then you must know Covington quite well.
PENNY. We've become pretty good friends.
CLARENCE. Just out of curiosity, you wouldn't know if he'd just hired a new secretary, would you?
PENNY. Why do you ask?
CLARENCE. Because I noticed something very odd about his letter. Look at this. *(HE holds the letter out for Penny to inspect.)* The woman has misspelled his name. See—Covinton. She typed it without the "G."
PENNY. (*Surprised.*) She certainly did.
CLARENCE. If she were new, then maybe—
PENNY. That's no excuse, Mr. Olander. A secretary ought to be able to spell her employer's name. Unless, of course, she works for an incredibly large East European law firm.

(CLARENCE misses the joke.)

CLARENCE. (*Plowing ahead.*) Well, I'm sure that by now he's already discovered the problem and has taken the necessary steps to correct it, so we'll just move on to other more important matters. (*HE puts the letter away and takes out another piece of paper.*) This morning I was finally able to give your résumé a careful read-through, and there were a couple of things I noticed which I'd like to ask you about.

PENNY. No misspellings, I hope.

CLARENCE. I don't think—(*The humor hits him late. A weak smile:*) No, of course not. (*Back to the business at hand:*) I just had a question or two about this series of very short periods of employment. For example, your tenure at Oakwood Elementary School in Lexington, Kentucky: September 3 to September 19 of [89].

PENNY.Yes?

CLARENCE. Well, it's not a complete school year.

PENNY. Nowhere near.

CLARENCE. And the year before—Hansen Elementary, Fort Worth, Texas. September 4 - September 17. That wasn't even two weeks.

PENNY. No, it wasn't.

CLARENCE. Forgive me for being blunt, Penny, but you weren't dismissed from these schools were you?

PENNY. Oh no. Quite the contrary.

CLARENCE. You quit.

PENNY. Yes.

CLARENCE. For what reasons?

PENNY. I employ teaching methods which are still fairly controversial, Mr. Olander. They're not yet meeting with widespread acceptance.

CLARENCE. (*Thinks he understands.*) Would that more of our schools followed the Covington model.

PENNY. The principals at Oakwood and Hansen—they hadn't the faintest idea of what it was I was trying to do. We came to loggerheads very early on. So rather than spend the entire school year battling it out with school administrators, I just cut my losses and said my goodbyes. I know that must seem like the coward's way out—

CLARENCE. Not at all.

PENNY. You mean that?

(MYRTLE gets up from her desk.)

CLARENCE. (*Nodding.*) The fact that you stuck it out for as long as you did—that should count for something too. Covington touched on the importance of these little victories in the paper he delivered to last year's Alternatives in Education Conference. Were you there?

PENNY. No. I think I was sick that week.

CLARENCE. But surely he sent you a copy.

PENNY. Oh yes. Two in fact.

CLARENCE. I think it's some of his best work since—(*Thinking.*) Tip of my tongue. His best work since what?

PENNY. *Why Can't Johnny Behave?*

CLARENCE. No. Even before that.

MYRTLE. (*Crossing into Clarence's office area.*) Clarence—

CLARENCE. Something to do with strict nuns.

MYRTLE. Clarence—

CLARENCE. What?

MYRTLE. I thought maybe I should take Penny upstairs to see her classroom. I mean before it gets too hot up there.

CLARENCE. All right.

(HE stands up. PENNY takes this as her cue to stand also.)

CLARENCE. Thank you for dropping by, Penny. I know you're going to be a real asset to Graceland.
PENNY. I'm looking forward to teaching here, Mr. Olander. And thank you for the soda.

(MYRTLE takes the can from PENNY and leads her into an implied hallway between the office and the classroom.)

MYRTLE. You'll be in Room 211. I should tell you that this classroom is not in the best of locations.
PENNY. What do you mean?
MYRTLE. For one thing, you've got Richard right next door to you in 209.
PENNY. Richard is the ex-marine?
MYRTLE. Yes, and a barker.
PENNY. A what?
MYRTLE. A barker. The man doesn't speak—he barks. Sounds like words are coming right up out of his stomach. Then on the other side of you is Doris Crumley.
PENNY. What's wrong with her?
MYRTLE. Nothing if you like to listen to a woman hitting things all day long—slapping her ruler on her desk, pounding on the blackboard. The kids are nervous wrecks by the end of the day. Let's hope you don't end up being one too. Come on. Let's go upstairs.

(PENNY *doesn't move. HER eye is drawn to something a few yards ahead of her. SHE makes a face.*)

MYRTLE. Isn't that just about the most godawful picture of him you've ever seen?

PENNY. Even at his heaviest, I don't think he looked *that* fat.

MYRTLE. I tried to talk Clarence out of having it done. He just insisted. It didn't seem right that a school named Graceland didn't have a life-size likeness of Elvis up on one of its walls. So he hired a little near-sighted man who does mosaics.

PENNY. Is that a guitar?

MYRTLE. Supposed to be. Except in all this heat so many of the colored tiles have fallen off it's starting to look more like a sickle or something. (*SHE steps back to get a better look.*) Elvis Presley, big and fat, holding a Communist sickle between his legs. And lucky us—we get to look at him all day long.

(*THEY go into the classroom as LIGHTS come up here.*)

MYRTLE. What do you think?

PENNY. It's all right.

MYRTLE. These desks are ancient. Clarence and I have been trying to get them replaced for years. (*SHE goes up to the student desk and runs her hand underneath the writing board.*) There's gum under here so old it's become petrified.

PENNY. (*Smiles.*) These are just like the ones I used to sit in back in Buffalo. (*SHE sits down in the desk.*)

MYRTLE. Could be the very same ones. The school purchasing office has a reputation for buying second hand.

(THEY both laugh. CLARENCE sniffs the air; something isn't right. HE gets up from his desk and crosses to Myrtle's desk.)

MYRTLE. I do hope you'll like it here, Penny—but not for the reasons Clarence thinks you will.
PENNY. What do you mean?

(CLARENCE is now coughing and fanning the air in front of his face.)

MYRTLE. All those things you said down in his office. I couldn't help overhearing—were they—I mean, did you mean all that, or were you just telling him what he wanted to hear?

(Before Penny can answer, CLARENCE's voice booms out over the public address system.)

CLARENCE. *(Into p.a. microphone.)* MYRTLE!
MYRTLE. *(Annoyed.)* Oh why does he—*(Addressing the unseen speaker box.)* WHAT?
CLARENCE. THERE'S DIRT BLOWING OUT OF YOUR FLOOR VENT. I CAN'T CLOSE IT.
MYRTLE. Turn the thing to the right. *(To Penny.)* He's totally helpless without me.
CLARENCE. IT'S NOT WORKING.
MYRTLE. I'm coming! *(To Penny.)* I've got to—
PENNY. I understand.

MYRTLE. Now you *will* do what I suggested—check yourself into a nice cool motel room until they get your power turned on.

PENNY. All right.

MYRTLE. And take a good long nap. You're going to need all the rest you can get during the next two days; the first week of school is a killer.

PENNY. Yes, thank you for the advice.

(MYRTLE goes. PENNY remains seated in the child's desk for a moment, thinking, then stands up and strolls slowly and thoughtfully around the room. SHE goes to the teacher's desk and sits down. SHE takes a bright red apple out of her bag and sets it down on the desk. SHE considers the apple for a moment, a pleased expression on her face. As SHE looks at the apple SHE begins to nod sleepily, her head finally falling with a thud onto the desk. LIGHTS dim slightly here as a BLUE LIGHT comes up elsewhere on stage illuminating MS. DANLEY marching in place.)

MS. DANLEY. Left-right, left-right. You-don't-want-to-get-left, right? Hup, two, three, four. We'll march till we drop, then we'll march some more.

(The BLUE LIGHT fades out. PENNY wakes up. It takes a moment for her to realize where she is. SHE then takes a hard look at the apple, turns and hurls it at the blackboard behind her. SHE then digs down into her bag and pulls up a pineapple. SHE plops it down on the desk and grins. BLACKOUT. We hear a few bars of Elvis singing "Don't Be Cruel.")

DAY TWO

(The MUSIC fades out as LIGHTS come up in Clarence's inner and outer offices. CLARENCE is sitting at his desk, talking on the phone. HE is sweating profusely, his tie is loosened, his sleeves rolled up.)

CLARENCE. Do you have any idea when he'll be back? ... Yes, very important. The fans aren't here. It's a quarter past eight and the fans Mr. Richter promised would be here, aren't— ... What do you mean "What kind of fans?" Fans with blades that go round and round, you stupid idiot. ... I'm sorry. I didn't mean to call you a stupid— ... I said I was sorry, Ms. Priddly. Look, we have no air conditioning. It's very hot in here and it's making us all a little crazy. Will you please ask Superintendent Richter to find out what happened? Maybe they were delivered to the wrong school. Will you do that? Thank you.

(HE hangs up. MYRTLE enters the outer office wearing a different pair of shorts and different summer blouse.)

CLARENCE. Is that *you*, Myrtle?
MYRTLE. Good *morning*, Clarence. *(SHE crosses to his desk.)*
CLARENCE. Where have you been?
MYRTLE. There was an accident on the interstate. Traffic was backed up for over a mile. It's like "The Road

Warrior" out there, Clarence. The heat is turning everyone into complete savages.

CLARENCE. I just called Miss Priddly a stupid idiot.

MYRTLE. She *is* a stupid idiot.

CLARENCE. She's going to tell Richter. I know it.

MYRTLE. What's he going to do—*fire* you?

CLARENCE. He's fired people for less than that before.

MYRTLE. Well, let's say he *does* fire you—...

CLARENCE. Oh God.

MYRTLE. ... It won't be the end of the world, Clarence. We can just go off and start that little school you and Vivian and I always used to talk about.

CLARENCE. That wasn't my idea. It was yours and Vivian's.

MYRTLE. It was just as much yours as ours. (*Beat.*) Your veins are bulging.

CLARENCE. What?

MYRTLE. The veins in your head are bulging out. I know that means you have a headache. Come on, let me give you a neck massage. (*SHE leads him out to her desk and sits him down in her chair. SHE positions her hands to begin the massage, but is obviously repelled by the perspiration and pulls away.*)

CLARENCE. The fans aren't here. Do you think I should send all the kids home?

MYRTLE. We can't do that. Most of their parents have already gone on to work.

CLARENCE. (*After a beat.*) Weren't you going to give me a neck rub?

MYRTLE. (*Apologetically.*) Your pores are really squirting it, honey.

(RICHARD WINGFIELD enters. HE is wearing slacks, long-sleeved shirt and very loosened tie. HE takes a long look at Clarence before speaking.)

RICHARD. You look like shit, sir.

MYRTLE. He's a nervous wreck, Richard. Don't pick on him.

RICHARD. I take it the air conditioning is still out.

MYRTLE. *(Sarcastic.)* No, Richard, we just thought it would be fun to set the thermostat at ninety degrees for a while.

RICHARD. You two are in wonderful moods this morning.

CLARENCE. We don't know what to do with all the kids.

RICHARD. I thought the idea was to bring them into the school and teach them.

MYRTLE. *(To Richard.)* You're not listening. It's ninety—*(Checking a thermometer on her desk.)*—one degrees in here.

RICHARD. Ninety-one is an autumn breeze compared to the summer I spent in the jungles of Grenada.

CLARENCE. We don't want to hear about it.

RICHARD. *(Ignoring him.)* Air so thick it was like walking through Campbell's soup.

MYRTLE. These are *kids*, Richard!

CLARENCE. Kids with parents who could sue our pants off if one of them got heat stroke or something.

*(DORIS CRUMLEY makes her entrance by slamming
HER ruler down on her clipboard. SHE wears a long-
sleeved blouse and a heavy looking skirt.)*

DORIS. I do not see my fan. I have been *to* my room
and there is no fan. I will not teach unless I have some
form of ventilation up there.
MYRTLE. The fans haven't arrived yet, Doris.
DORIS. Why? Why haven't they arrived?
CLARENCE. I'm trying to find out.
DORIS. When you do find out, I shall be in the lounge.
(SHE exits.)
RICHARD. 'Woman reminds me of a yip-yapping little
poodle. Permission to muzzle her, sir?
MYRTLE. *(To Richard.)* You haven't seen Penny yet,
have you?
RICHARD. Who's Penny?
MYRTLE. The new teacher. Took Angela's section.
RICHARD. What does she look like?
MYRTLE. About medium height—
RICHARD. [Brown] hair, kind of [straight]?
MYRTLE. Right.
RICHARD. Nice looking?
MYRTLE. Yes.
RICHARD. *(Crossing to the window.)* There's a
woman fitting that description out on the sidewalk in front
of the school. She's got a big crowd of kids around her.
CLARENCE. What's she doing?
RICHARD. Cooking breakfast, looks like.
MYRTLE. Breakfast? *(SHE joins him at the window.)*
RICHARD. Spatula in one hand, carton of eggs in the
other.

MYRTLE. He's right, Clarence. Oh, this is so cute. She's frying eggs right on the sidewalk. Just like when they say—
CLARENCE. I *know* what they say, Myrtle.
RICHARD. New teach sounds like a lot of fun, sir.
CLARENCE. Strictly a scientific experiment, I'm sure.

(The PHONE rings. CLARENCE motions for Myrtle to answer it. SHE ignores him. HE sighs and picks it up.)

CLARENCE. Graceland. ... Hi, Bernie. ... Great. We'll be down in a minute. (*HE hangs up. To Richard.*) Bernie says the fans just arrived. They're unloading them in the back. You want to give me a hand? (*HE exits.*)
RICHARD. (*To Myrtle.*) Lot of fun, good looker—and we all thought poor Angela could never be replaced.

(His parting leer out the window is met by a very disapproving look from MYRTLE. As HE leaves, SHE refocuses on the activity outside.)

MYRTLE. (*As if Penny could hear her.*) You are so clever, Penny—entertaining the kids by frying eggs on the—(*A beat, puzzled.*) What's with the bacon, honey?

(A school BELL RINGS, then BLACKOUT. LIGHTS come up in Penny's classroom. PENNY stands facing the class. SHE wears an apron over a light summer dress.)

PENNY. (*Taking off the apron.*) Good morning, children. For those of you I didn't meet outside, I am your teacher for the year—Penny Patterson. (*SHE writes the name on the board and turns back to her students.*) I am new to Graceland this year, but I certainly am not new to teaching. I have been a teacher for twelve years. That's a dozen. (*SHE finds and holds up an empty egg carton.*) Now, here's an interesting fact about me which you all should know: I believe in a totally free and uncluttered learning environment. What does that mean? Well, for starters it means we get rid of these desks. So let's pull everything out of our desks. All your books, all your tablets and pencils, your cute little plastic purses. I want everything piled up against that wall over there. (*SHE watches as her students follow her instructions.*) And when you finish I want you to return to your desks and join me in a few arm and waist stretches. (*SHE removes her apron and begins stretching.*) Tippy toe, tippy toe, tickle the clouds with your fingertips. Now we are a pendulum. Tick tock like a clock. Back and forth, back and forth. (*SHE lets her arms go limp, bends over and swings them monkey-like in a half arc.*) Okay. Let's shake it out. (*SHE shakes her arms, and crosses to the student desk.*) Very good. Now, boys and girls, I want each of you to squat beside your desks, and grab hold, bending at the knees so as not to overtax our formative, young back muscles. Now, let's lift our desks ... (*SHE picks up the desk.*) ... right up off the floor. Not so heavy without the books inside, now is it? Okay, with a firm grip—(*Seeing trouble.*)—somebody help the little one over there. She's about to lose it. (*SHE waits for the momentary crisis to pass.*) With a firm grip on our desks, let's carry them single-file over to the two windows whose panes I removed earlier this morning. Please stay away from that pile of broken glass in the corner there.

(*SHE carries the desk across the room.*) And does anybody know what we're going to do with these desks when we get to the windows? Very good! (*SHE hurls the desk off stage.*) Down, down, down. Such a liberating sound—the crack and clatter of wood on wood!

(*BLACKOUT. LIGHTS come up in Clarence's office. CLARENCE sits hunched over his desk sifting and sorting. HE reaches absently for his nut bowl and knocks it off the desk.*)

CLARENCE. Damn it all to hell!

(*HE gets up, crosses to where the nut bowl lies, and begins to put the scattered nuts back in the bowl. MYRTLE rushes in.*)

MYRTLE. (*Urgently.*) Clarence—
CLARENCE. Don't crunch them! Watch where you're—
MYRTLE. We have a serious problem, Clarence. Get up. (*SHE goes to look out Clarence's window.*) Come here.

(*With great reluctance HE pulls himself to his feet and walks over to where Myrtle is standing. SHE points something out to him.*)

MYRTLE. There goes another one.

(*CLARENCE blinks a couple of times. It's obviously hard for him to accept what he's seeing.*)

CLARENCE. Whose classroom is that?
MYRTLE. It could be Penny's. Or Richard's. I can't—
CLARENCE. (*To himself.*) This doesn't make any—
(*To Myrtle.*) What are you waiting for? Find out who it is.

(*LIGHTS come up in the outer office as MYRTLE crosses
to her desk.*)

CLARENCE. I want that teacher in my office, Myrtle.
Immediately.

(*HE remains at the window, staring out in stunned
disbelief. MYRTLE picks up the p.a. microphone. For
a moment SHE doesn't seem to know what to say.
Finally, SHE clears her throat and speaks into the mike,
her voice noticeably amplified.*)

MYRTLE.
YOUR ATTENTION
PLEASE. MAY I HAVE
YOUR ATTENTION
PLEASE? WILL THE
TEACHER WHOSE
STUDENTS ARE
THROWING THEIR
DESKS OUT THE
WINDOW, PLEASE
REPORT TO MR.
OLANDER'S OFFICE—
IMMEDIATELY.

CLARENCE.
(*To himself.*) Not the
p.a. system. Did I say to
broadcast this all over the
damn school? (*HE goes to
Myrtle.*)

CLARENCE. (*To Myrtle.*) What in God's name are you doing?

(*Before MYRTLE can respond, the PHONE on her desk rings. SHE answers it quickly. SHE is still pushing the button on the p.a. microphone, so the first few words of her phone conversation are also amplified.*)

MYRTLE. Graceland Elementary School. Clarence Olander's office.

(*CLARENCE yanks the microphone away from her.*)

MYRTLE. Yes. Just a moment. (*Covering the mouthpiece.*) It's Boozer from next door. (*MYRTLE hands the phone to CLARENCE.*)

CLARENCE. This is Clarence Olander. ... No, Mr. Boosler, nobody's planning a bonfire, I assure— ... Yes, we are most certainly getting to the bottom of it. (*To Myrtle.*) Would you please go up there and—(*Into phone.*) That's impossible. There isn't a child in this school strong enough to hurl a desk—(*To Myrtle.*) Why are you just standing there?
MYRTLE. You're on my foot.

(*DORIS enters.*)

CLARENCE. (*Into phone.*) Something else must have hit your Impala.
DORIS. (*To Myrtle.*) It's the new one.

CLARENCE. (*Overlapping, into phone.*) How the hell should *I*—?

MYRTLE. (*Overlapping, to Doris.*)What?

CLARENCE. (*Overlapping, into phone.*) You go right ahead and sue, you spiteful old son of a—(*Mr. Boosler has hung up.*)

DORIS. (*Overlapping.*) The new teacher. The one who took Angela's place. (*Looking out the window.*) Would you look—they are destroying all the beautiful shrubbery!

(*CLARENCE hands the phone receiver back to MYRTLE for her to hang up.*)

CLARENCE. (*To Doris.*) You're saying those desks are coming from Ms. Patterson's classroom?

DORIS. Can't you see? There she is. That's her— leaning out the window.

CLARENCE. (*Tilting his glasses.*) God, I need new glasses. (*To Myrtle.*) What's she doing?

MYRTLE. She's waving at us. (*Waving back.*) Hi, Penny! (*SHE motions for Penny to come down to the office.*) I think she saw me.

(*RICHARD enters.*)

RICHARD. (*To Myrtle.*) You said somebody's throwing computer disks out the window?

MYRTLE. Not disks, Richard. *Desks.*

RICHARD. Disks, desks—who found a way to get the damn windows open?

CLARENCE. Would you please just go on back to your classrooms—both of you? Myrtle, make them go back to their classrooms. (*HE grabs his head in pain.*)
MYRTLE. We'll handle this. Go on now.

(*SHE gently nudges Doris toward the door. DORIS swats Myrtle on the bottom with her ruler.*)

DORIS. Do not touch me! Nobody touches me!
PENNY. (*Enters. To Clarence.*) You wanted to see me? (*To Myrtle.*) Hello, Myrtle.
MYRTLE. (*Awkwardly.*) Hello, Penny.
PENNY. (*To Doris.*) I don't believe we've met. I'm Penny Patterson.

(*DORIS gawks at Penny without speaking. RICHARD steps forward and takes Penny's hand.*)

RICHARD. Richard Wingfield. 209.
PENNY. (*Pleasantly.*) Oh yes.
RICHARD. You have beautiful eyes, Penny Patterson. Doe eyes.
PENNY. That's very sweet.
CLARENCE. (*Moves in between Penny and Richard.*) Would all of you just go? Would you please just GO?

(*As RICHARD, DORIS and PENNY start to leave:*)

CLARENCE. Not you, Penny. You stay.

(*HE steers PENNY into his inner office. MYRTLE follows.*)

CLARENCE. (*To Myrtle, over his shoulder:*) Hold my calls.

MYRTLE. But I really think I should be in on—
CLARENCE. (*Interrupting.*) I want to see Penny *alone*, Myrtle. And I don't want to be disturbed.

(*MYRTLE at first seems ready to argue, but then gives up and exits in a huff, knocking the phone receiver out of its cradle on her desk on her way out.*)

CLARENCE. Please, Penny—sit down.

(*PENNY sits down. CLARENCE paces.*)

CLARENCE. Penny—
PENNY. (*Interrupting.*) I know what I did was wrong, Mr. Olander. I will gladly pay to have all the desks replaced.
CLARENCE. One of the neighbors said a desk struck his car.
PENNY. Not the whole desk. Just the seat. I will pay for the damage, Mr. Olander. I have a little money set aside.

(*A beat. CLARENCE is thinking.*)

PENNY. It's a very old car. (*SHE stands up.*) May I— May I go now?

(CLARENCE shakes his head. PENNY sits back down. CLARENCE takes a moment to put words to his thoughts.)

CLARENCE. Penny—
PENNY. Yes?
CLARENCE. Did you tell the children to throw their desks out the window?
PENNY. Yes, I did.
CLARENCE. Why?
PENNY. I don't know. Just a sudden impulse, I guess.
CLARENCE. How often do you get these sudden impulses?
PENNY. Never. Well, hardly ever.
CLARENCE. Some little light just went off in your head?
PENNY. I suppose you could say that.
CLARENCE. Are you feeling all right, Penny?
PENNY. I don't know. I guess so.
CLARENCE. Would you like to go home?
PENNY. Oh no. I couldn't possibly go home. You know how important it is for a teacher to be with her students on the first day of school.

(MYRTLE enters with a couple of cans of soda. SHE hands one to Penny.)

PENNY. Thank you very much.

(MYRTLE takes a big long drink before giving the second can to Clarence.)

MYRTLE. (*Looking Penny over.*) You don't look well, honey. How did you sleep over the weekend?

CLARENCE. (*A dismissal:*) Thank you, Myrtle.

PENNY. (*Rising.*) Please, Mr. Olander. I give you my word it won't happen again. (*To Myrtle.*) It was just that I thought we should all sit on the floor. You know how kids love to sit on the floor.

MYRTLE. Like Indians.

PENNY. Yes.

CLARENCE. We don't play Indians in this school, Penny.

PENNY. If the floor turned out to be too hard I was going to make little pillows for the children.

MYRTLE. Oh, Penny, honey—you have so many little talents!

CLARENCE. (*To Penny.*) If it was so important for you and the children to sit on the floor, what was wrong with simply pushing the desks up against the wall?

PENNY. (*Takes a long time to answer.*) Well, they would still be there, wouldn't they? In the classroom. Where we could see them.

CLARENCE. The desks *offended* you?

PENNY. No—It's just that it seemed very important to be rid of them. In a permanent sort of way.

CLARENCE. Would you please tell me what any of this has to do with the Covington method?

PENNY. It goes to the heart of one of Covington's most recent theories. Very complicated—I haven't time to go into it right now.

MYRTLE. She said she was sorry, Clarence. She said she would pay for everything. Didn't you, honey?

(PENNY nods.)

MYRTLE. And besides—you're always saying how we need to get rid of those ugly desks. Now maybe Richter will do what he promised us he was going to do two years ago and get us some new ones.

CLARENCE. Penny, would you mind waiting outside for a moment?

MYRTLE. *(To Penny.)* You go on back to your classroom, honey.

CLARENCE. *(To Myrtle.)* I'd *like* her to—

MYRTLE. *(To Clarence.)* She can wait just as easily in her classroom. *(To Penny.)* Go on, now.

(PENNY looks at Clarence. HE capitulates.)

PENNY. Thank you, Mr. Olander. *(To Myrtle, more heartfelt.)* Thank you. *(PENNY leaves.)*

CLARENCE. *(Waits until Penny is out of ear-shot. Then:)* Don't you ever do that again.

MYRTLE. Do what?

CLARENCE. You know what you did.

MYRTLE. No I don't.

CLARENCE. You undermined my authority right in front of one of the teachers.

MYRTLE. It certainly wasn't intentional.

CLARENCE. Don't do it again. *(HE looks out the window.)* And ask Mr. Mattson to haul away those desks. It looks like a trash dump out there.

MYRTLE. Your wish is my command! *(MYRTLE bows her way out of the office.)*

CLARENCE. (*Digs around in the clutter on his desk for something. HE finds it—a piece of paper with a phone number on it. HE dials.*) Yes, this is Clarence Olander. I'm the principal at Graceland Elementary School in Springdale. ... Graceland, right. ... That's right. I'd like to speak to Mr. Covington if he's in. ... Well, do you think he can give me a call when he gets back in town? It's rather important. ... Well, it concerns someone who used to work for him—Penny Patterson. ... Just a moment. Let me find her résumé. (*HE digs out the résumé.*) She was one of his research assistants about—about thirteen years ago, but I understand they've stayed in touch. ... Yes. Clarence Olander. 555-9896. Thank you very much. (*HE hangs up. HE studies the résumé for a moment. Something disturbs him. Reading from the résumé aloud:*) "Research assistant, Fall, [1979] through Spring [1980] for author/educator... R. J.—(*Stops, looks up.*) God, how did I miss this? She's misspelled his—She's left out the "G"!

(*CLARENCE stares ahead, a look of deep concern on his face as LIGHTS slowly fade out here. LIGHTS come up dim elsewhere on stage. PENNY is alone, walking through the school corridors on her way back to her students. SHE stops, her mind wandering back to a classroom from her childhood. The classroom area is slowly illuminated by soft BLUE LIGHT. MS. DANLEY sits behind the teacher's desk. The school BELL RINGS. SHE silently begins to take roll.*)

MS. DANLEY. (*Looking about.*) Penny Patterson? Where is Penny Patterson?

PENNY. I'm coming! (*SHE crosses quickly to the classroom. To Ms. Danley.*) Sorry I'm late.

(*SHE settles into the empty desk. MS. DANLEY sees something elsewhere in the room which displeases her.*)

MS. DANLEY. Beverly, are you aware that you're sitting in Carolyn's seat?
BEVERLY'S VOICE. Yes, ma'am.
MS. DANLEY. Did I give you permission to sit in Carolyn's seat while she was away?
BEVERLY'S VOICE. No, ma'am.
MS. DANLEY. Then why are you sitting there?
BEVERLY'S VOICE. My desk has a splinter in it.
MS.DANLEY. A splinter. Do you think you're the first child in the history of the world who ever had to sit on a splinter?
BEVERLY'S VOICE. No, ma'am.
MS. DANLEY. Then I would suggest you move back to your assigned seat and show a little grit. In my day a tiny splinter would have meant nothing compared to all the other sacrifices to personal comfort we were called upon to make. Sacrifices we were more than *willing* to make because that's how much we valued our education!
BEVERLY'S VOICE. But it *hurts*.
MS. DANLEY. Are you sassing me, missy?
BEVERLY'S VOICE. No.
MS. DANLEY. No what?
BEVERLY'S VOICE. No, ma'am.
MS. DANLEY. Then move your prickled little bottom into your assigned seat and shut up. And I would suggest you bring a little sandpaper with you to school tomorrow.

BEVERLY'S VOICE. Yes, ma'am.

MS. DANLEY. Has anyone seen Bobby? (*No response.*) Kevin—you live next door to Bobby. Have they brought him home from the hospital yet?

KEVIN'S VOICE. Yes, ma'am.

MS. DANLEY. Did anyone say when he'd be ready to come back to school?

KEVIN'S VOICE. I don't know.

MS. DANLEY. When did you see him?

KEVIN'S VOICE. Yesterday.

MS. DANLEY. Did he seem well?

KEVIN'S VOICE. I don't know.

MS. DANLEY. What was he doing when you saw him? (*KEVIN doesn't answer.*) Answer the question, young man. What was Bobby doing when you saw him?

KEVIN'S VOICE. I can't say.

MS. DANLEY. Why can't you say?

KEVIN'S VOICE. He said if I told you he'd beat me up.

MS. DANLEY. Beat you up?

KEVIN'S VOICE. Yes. Break my legs and make putty out of my face.

MS. DANLEY. Do you think he would really do that, Kevin?

KEVIN'S VOICE. Yes, ma'am.

MS. DANLEY. Who are you more afraid of, Kevin—Bobby or me?

KEVIN'S VOICE. You.

MS. DANLEY. You what?

KEVIN'S VOICE. You, ma'am.

MS. DANLEY. So tell me what it was that Bobby was doing if he wasn't in bed recuperating from his tonsillectomy.
KEVIN'S VOICE. He was throwing darts—
MS. DANLEY. Go on.
KEVIN'S VOICE. He was throwing darts at a picture of your face.

(PENNY bursts out laughing.)

MS. DANLEY. You find this amusing, Penny?
PENNY. *(Trying desperately to suppress it.)* No.
MS. DANLEY. Stand up, Penny.

(PENNY stands, still choking back laughter.)

MS. DANLEY. You don't find the idea of throwing darts at teacher's face the least bit funny? *(PENNY shakes her head.)* Then what is it that's gotten you so tickled, young lady?
PENNY. Nothing.
MS. DANLEY. You just like to laugh for no reason.
PENNY. No. Yes.
MS. DANLEY. Go to the blackboard, Penny.

(PENNY goes to the blackboard. MS. DANLEY hands her a piece of chalk.)

MS. DANLEY. I want you to write "I am a hyena" fifty times. And I don't want you to stop laughing until you finish. Now, of course, if at any point you want to stop acting like a hyena and start acting like a little girl, then we'll all be happy to hear what it was you found so terribly funny just now. So go ahead, Penny—be a hyena.

(*PENNY now begins to laugh in a very forced, mechanical manner: heh, heh, heh, etc. SHE writes "I am a ..." stops, struggles with the spelling of the word hyena, finally settling on H-I-E-E-N-A. SHE turns to Ms. Danley. DANLEY shakes her head. PENNY erases.*)

MS. DANLEY. (*Dictating.*) Hyena. H-Y-E-N-A. Hyena. (*To class, as PENNY begins writing and laughing again.*) Now, let's turn in our social studies books to Chapter 17: "Africa, the Dark Continent."

(*LIGHTS fade to black. We hear a few bars of Elvis singing "In the Ghetto."*)

DAY THREE

(*MUSIC fades out as LIGHTS come up over Clarence and Myrtle's desks. CLARENCE sits at his desk. The tie is completely gone now. HE now wears a short-sleeved shirt comfortably unbuttoned around the neck. MYRTLE enters, dressed in her usual summer apparel.*)

MYRTLE. Good morning, Clarence.
CLARENCE. Come in here, Myrtle.
MYRTLE. (*As SHE goes into the inner office.*) Good morning, Clarence.

CLARENCE. (*Preoccupied.*) Good morning, good morning. Look at this. (*HE hands Myrtle a piece of paper from his desk.*) I didn't get any sleep last night.

MYRTLE. (*Shrugging.*) It's Penny's résumé.

CLARENCE. Tell me what's wrong with it.

MYRTLE. Somebody spilled a little Pepsi or something in the corner.

CLARENCE. Not that, Myrtle. *Read it.* Read the first entry under "Employment History."

MYRTLE. Oh dear. A lot of people seem to have trouble spelling that name, don't they?

CLARENCE. I tried to reach Covington yesterday. His secretary said he was out of town but promised to have him call me as soon as he got back. Look at the letter of recommendation, Myrtle. (*HE hands her the recommendation letter.*) She didn't even bother to type them on different typewriters.

MYRTLE. If what you're implying is true, Clarence, then you've got to wonder what it is about Graceland that appeals to her so much. I mean, pretending to respect the work of R.J. Covington is not an easy thing to—

CLARENCE. *I* respect Covington's work, Myrtle. I respect his work very much.

(*MYRTLE gives Clarence a very skeptical look.*)

CLARENCE. I hate it when you look at me that way. Don't look at me that way.

MYRTLE. The Clarence Olander I used to know would have never looked up to a man who thinks elementary schools should be run like reformatories.

CLARENCE. That is not what Covington is saying.

MYRTLE. He's a jerk, Clarence. Just like Superintendent Richter is a jerk. Just like half the teachers you've hired here in the three years you've been principal have been jerks. Jerks and jerkettes. I don't know why you don't see it. Vivian would have seen it. She would have pointed it out to you in that sweet, funny, crazy way of hers and you would have listened.

(*LIGHTS come up on PENNY in her classroom. SHE wears a white dress with a pattern of various breeds of dogs on it—some barking, some chewing bones and so forth.*)

PENNY. (*Addressing her class.*) Good morning, children. My, my—look at all the smiling faces.

(*CLARENCE and MYRTLE stare at one another in silence, both with totally unsmiling faces. Finally:*)

MYRTLE. I've got to have a Pepsi.

(*MYRTLE goes out, leaving CLARENCE alone with his thoughts as LIGHTS fade out here.*)

PENNY. (*Leaning casually against the edge of her desk.*) Today is what we call a "dog day." Does anybody know what we mean by that? Well, a dog day is a very hot day—a hot, sticky day where nothing moves—even the air itself just kind of hangs there all thick and gooey. And who knows how "dog day" got it's name? (*No takers.*) I'll give you the official reason first. Dog days were originally called "dog *star* days." They were called that because they usually come late in the summer when the dog star, called Sirius, rises and sets with the sun.

(DORIS now appears in the hallway, clipboard and ruler in hand. SHE stands watching Penny disapprovingly. PENNY will not be aware of her.)

PENNY. Now I'll give you what I think is a much better reason: ever seen a dog on a hot day? The way he just kind of lies around, his tongue hanging out, all droopy-faced—no manners whatsoever! Well, that's the way a dog day makes you feel—like a lazy old hound dog. Let's all be lazy old hound dogs for a moment. *(SHE climbs up on her desk and sprawls out across the top of it. SHE lets her whole body go limp. SHE opens her mouth and sticks out her tongue, then begins to pant in short puffs like a dog. In between pants:)* Now, Nichole, I know you can do better than that. Sarah, Kimberly—show Nichole what to do with her paws. Good girl!

(DORIS cannot contain herself any longer. While Penny's back is still turned, SHE blusters into the classroom and slaps her clipboard with her ruler. PENNY turns with a start.)

DORIS. May I ask the meaning of all this?
PENNY. *(Cheerfully.)* Hello, Ms. Crumley. *(Confidentially, almost a whisper.)* You're in the wrong classroom, Ms. Crumley. Yours is one door down.
DORIS. Just who do you think you are ... *(Slap.)* ... coming in here dressed like that and playing these silly games. This is not in the curriculum.

PENNY. Sometimes my lesson plans diverge a little.

DORIS. A *little*? (*Slap.*) A *little*? (*Slap.*)

PENNY. Please don't do that in my classroom, Ms. Crumley. It disturbs the children.

DORIS. I want to know who you are. (*Slap.*) I want to know where you came from!

(*DORIS is poised to slap the ruler again, but PENNY catches her arm.*)

PENNY. This really isn't the best time ... (*SHE gives Doris's arm a little twist, then plucks the ruler from Doris's grasp.*) ... for us to be having ... (*SHE breaks the ruler over her knee.*) ... this little chat. Perhaps we should get together ... (*SHE tosses the pieces of the broken ruler on the floor.*) ... some other time, okay?

(*DORIS is in a temporary state of shock.*)

PENNY. *Okay?*

DORIS. You broke my—

PENNY. Yes, I know. I'm afraid you don't have a license for that thing, Ms. Crumley. Now if you'd just run along—(*SHE gestures for Doris to leave.*) Say goodbye to Ms. Crumley, children.

DORIS. (*Malevolently.*) I'm going to get you for this, Penny Patterson. (*DORIS snatches up the pieces of her broken ruler.*)

PENNY. We should try to think kind thoughts around the children, Ms. Crumley.

DORIS. If Clarence isn't going to do anything about you I know someone who will. (*DORIS storms off.*)

PENNY. (*Returns to her desk.*) Now what just happened here, boys and girls? (*Listens.*) Well, yes—it is very possible that Ms. Crumley doesn't like dogs. And how do we feel about that? (*Listens.*) Yes. I'm afraid it makes us very sad. Because dogs deserve our affection just as much as people do. We should show our canine friends how we feel about this unfortunate situation.

(SHE climbs up on her desk, throws her head back and howls, very loudly, almost like a wolf or coyote. SHE encourages her students to do the same. LIGHTS snap on in Clarence's inner and outer offices. CLARENCE sits at his desk. HE hears the howling but can't determine where it's coming from. HE gets up to investigate and shuffles out. The offices are empty for a moment, then DORIS sneaks in, cases the rooms to make sure she's alone, then picks up the phone receiver on Myrtle's desk and dials. PENNY stops howling and gets down from the desk. CLARENCE appears in the hallway, pokes his head into a couple of the other classrooms, then looks in on Penny. SHE sees him at the door, gives him a little wave; everything seems okay in here. HE nods, moves on, turning a corner and disappearing.)

DORIS. (*Into phone.*) Superintendent Richter, please. ... This is Doris Crumley. I'm a teacher at Graceland Elementary School. ... I really need to speak to him, Ms. Priddly. There is something happening here at Graceland which I think he should be made aware of. ... No. I'd rather he not call me back here. Let me give you my home number. He can phone me tonight.

PENNY. (*Leans against the teacher's desk, addressing her students.*) Great Dane, Basset, Collie, Poodle, Golden Retriever, German Shepherd. Hey, let's not stop there— we've still got one hundred twenty-two breeds left to go!

(*FADE up Elvis Presley singing "Hound Dog" as all LIGHTS fade out.*)

END OF ACT I

ACT II

DAY FOUR

LIGHTS come up on PENNY sitting on top of her desk in her classroom. SHE wears a cartoonish-looking African tribeswoman ensemble—lots of colorful beads and bracelets, perhaps a wrap-around animal skin skirt. On her head is a crown made of animal bones. A portable tape recorder sits on the desk beside her. SHE addresses her class.

PENNY. Good morning, children. I bring you sad news about your teacher, Ms. Patterson. There has been a tragic accident out on the playground involving a hungry stray poodle, a box of dog biscuits, and two fingers on poor Penny's right hand. Before leaving for the minor emergency clinic she asked that I, one of her oldest and dearest friends, fill in for her until she is able to once again grip the chalk stick without muscular pain. Permit me, then, to introduce myself. I am—(*SHE goes to the blackboard and writes.*) She-rumba, Queen of the Congo. Let's all say the name together.

(*BLACKOUT. Jungle MUSIC plays. LIGHTS come up in Clarence's office. CLARENCE sits at his desk working. HE now wears a short-sleeved shirt and no tie. HE holds up two sheets of paper, one in each hand, and compares them.*)

CLARENCE. "F 17 B" and "F 17 C." It's the same damned form! You're burying me, Richter. You're burying me alive! (*HE lets his head fall to the desk, and in the process knocks the nut bowl onto the floor.*) Goddamnit!

(*HE gets up from the desk and goes to pick up the pistachios. We now see that HE is wearing shorts— loud, colorful bermudas. MYRTLE enters, stops at her desk to put her things away, then seeing Clarence crouched down in his shorts, SHE begins to laugh.*)

MYRTLE. Oh Clarence, you look adorable!
CLARENCE. I'm just being practical.
MYRTLE. Well, I could *practically* eat you up! Turn around and give me a little fashion show.
CLARENCE. I'm not modeling for you.

(*The TELEPHONE rings. MYRTLE picks it up at her desk.*)

MYRTLE. Graceland Elementary School. Good morning, Mr. Boosler.

(*SHE makes a disgusted face. CLARENCE shakes his head and waves his arms.*)

MYRTLE. He's not in, Mr. Boosler. I'll have him c— ... (*Covers the phone mouthpiece.*) He knows you're here, Clarence. He saw your car pull up about an hour ago.
CLARENCE. (*Sighs and takes the phone from Myrtle.*) Yes, Mr. Boosler, what can I do for you?

*(RICHARD enters. HE is wearing a t-shirt emblazoned
with the letters USMC and camouflage-patterned fatigue
pants.)*

RICHARD. *(Seeing Clarence's shorts.)* Why, look
who's here—It's Clarence's groovy twin brother!
CLARENCE. *(Into phone.)* You want to run that by
me again, please?
MYRTLE. *(To Richard.)* What are you doing down here?
The morning bell rang ten minutes ago.
RICHARD. Doris sent me down to remind you that
this is the morning her kids take the PTQSTAT and
nobody is to disturb her under any circumstances, or we
will all suffer the consequences.
MYRTLE. Thank you, Richard. We'll be sure to stay
out of her way.

(RICHARD exits.)

CLARENCE. *(Into phone.)* I find that just a little bit
hard to— ...
MYRTLE. *(To Clarence.)* What?
CLARENCE. How can you even *see* into her
classroom? You're all the way across the—
MYRTLE. What *is* it, Clarence?
CLARENCE. *(Into phone.)* You're a sick man, Boosler.
You ought to be put away. *(HE hangs up. To Myrtle.)*
He's been watching Penny's classroom with binoculars.
MYRTLE. And?
CLARENCE. He says she's dressed like the Queen of
Sheba. She's performing what look like ritualistic chants

and carrying things around the room between her elbows. (*Very long pause as all of this sinks in.*) Maybe you ought to go check on her, Myrtle.
MYRTLE. All right.
CLARENCE. (*Still thinking.*) Maybe you ought to bring her down to my office.
MYRTLE. Okay.

(*Suddenly we hear the sound of PENNY'S VOICE in its lowest register.*)

PENNY'S VOICE. Ooga chaka! Ooga chaka!
CLARENCE. Now, Myrtle! Now!

(*MYRTLE dashes out of the office. LIGHTS come up in Penny's classroom. PENNY, still dressed as She-rumba, stands on her chair which has been pulled out from behind her desk. SHE is singing.*)

PENNY. "Abba-dabba in monkey talk means chimp I love you too. Then the big baboon one night in June, ...

(*MYRTLE rushes in. PENNY sees her and gestures "just a moment."*)

PENNY. ... he married them and very soon, they went upon their abba dabba honeymoon." Hello, Myrtle.
MYRTLE. Penny?
PENNY. (*Correcting her.*) She-rumba.
MYRTLE. "She-rumba"?
PENNY. Queen of the Congo.
MYRTLE. Queen of the—

PENNY. (*Jumps down from her chair. To her class.*) I know—let's see how many books Ms. Dixon can hold between *her* elbows.

MYRTLE. Clarence wants to see you, Penny.

PENNY. Right now?

MYRTLE. Yes.

PENNY. Well, I don't know. I haven't even gotten started here yet.

MYRTLE. He really needs to see you, Penny.

PENNY. If it's important, then I will just have to go. (*To her class.*) She-rumba is going down the river to the "Land of the Many Elvis Pictures." She will be back just as soon as she can. Why don't you all work quietly on your African tribal headdresses? They're coming along very nicely!

(PENNY and MYRTLE leave the classroom as LIGHTS dim out here. On their way to Clarence's office, THEY pass Richard.)

RICHARD. (*Amused.*) Ooga *chaka!*

(PENNY smiles as MYRTLE escorts her into Clarence's inner office. CLARENCE tries very hard to conceal his astonishment over her outfit. HE stares at her for a moment without speaking.)

MYRTLE. Can I get anybody anything? She-rumba?

PENNY. No thank you.

(CLARENCE shakes his head. Another silence.)

PENNY. Those are very interesting shorts, Mr. Olander. (*Another pause, then.*)
CLARENCE. Hold my calls, Myrtle.

(*HE motions for Penny to sit down. SHE sits. MYRTLE goes out to her desk and pretends to be busy. Through the exchange which follows it will be obvious from her reactions that SHE is listening in.*)

CLARENCE. (*To Penny.*) All right. Time for an explanation.
PENNY. I'm sorry, Mr. Olander. I won't let it—
CLARENCE. Explanation, Penny. Not apology. Why are you dressed this way? Why did Myrtle call you "She-rambo"?
PENNY. (*Gently correcting.*) Not "Rambo." "Rumba." Like the dance. (*SHE strikes a dance-like pose.*)
CLARENCE. So you're not Penny Patterson any more.
PENNY. Yes.
CLARENCE. Yes, what?
PENNY. Yes sir?
CLARENCE. No. I mean clarify. Yes, you're not Penny?
PENNY. No. (*Confused.*) I mean yes. Yes, I *am* Penny.
CLARENCE. You just said you were—
PENNY. That's right.
CLARENCE. (*Calling.*) MYRTLE!
MYRTLE. (*Bounds up from her desk.*) What is it?
CLARENCE. I have a splitting headache.
MYRTLE. I'll get you something. (*SHE exits.*)
CLARENCE. (*Clawing his head.*) I'm trying to understand this, Penny.

PENNY. I really would like to get back to my children, Mr. Olander.

CLARENCE. You're not going back to your children, Penny.

PENNY. But they need me.

CLARENCE. They need a *teacher*. Someone who teaches. You're not teaching. You're up there chanting and carrying things between your elbows. (*Takes a deep breath.*) I'm going to start over and I would appreciate your cooperation.

PENNY. All right. You have my full cooperation.

CLARENCE. You are She-rumba—

PENNY. Yes, I am She-rumba. (*Beat.*) Queen of the Congo. Daughter of Donga-wonkie, granddaughter of Nah-Timba, Lord of the Tree People.

CLARENCE. The "Tree People"?

PENNY. (*Nodding.*) Who lived their entire lives high among the treetops of the tropical rain forest. Friends to the rainbow-plumed chatter-birds and the arboreal wise-monkeys.

CLARENCE. Oh Jesus God. MYRTLE!

MYRTLE. (*Rushes in with a bottle of aspirin and a glass of water.*) I'm coming! I'm coming! (*SHE trips over something and spills the glass of water in Clarence's lap.*)

CLARENCE. (*Leaping up.*) Good God!

MYRTLE. I'm sorry, Clarence. Really I am.

CLARENCE. It looks like I just peed on myself!

MYRTLE. (*Sincerely but a little tickled.*) Oh Clarence—now everybody's going to think you're having prostate trouble again.

CLARENCE. Would you just shut up, Myrtle? Would you just shut up and get out of here?

PENNY. I don't think you should talk to Myrtle that way, Mr. Olander.

MYRTLE. (*To Penny.*) It's okay, honey. He didn't mean it.

PENNY. (*To Clarence.*) I think you should apologize.

CLARENCE. What?

PENNY. In fact, I absolutely command you.

CLARENCE. (*Incredulous.*) You "command" me?

PENNY. (*Liking her newfound authoritarian manner.*) I order you this very instant.

CLARENCE. (*Sharing his disbelief with Myrtle.*) This has got to be the most—(*Turning back to Penny.*) Who is the principal here, Penny?

PENNY. (*On a roll.*) And from here on out I think it would be better if you addressed me only by my tribal name. I earned that name in battle, paid a heavy price for that name. We were ambushed, you see—struck numb by a sudden barrage of Mungahili petti-darts. Many of our warriors were left without full use of their limbs. We retreated from the Valley of Fire like this. (*SHE gets up and walks around the room on the sides of her feet, her arms flailing.*)

CLARENCE. For Christ's sake, Penny.

PENNY. It was a very full and eventful summer for me back in Africa. My elemental African summer.

CLARENCE. You don't stop, do you?

PENNY. I hope to return some day. Perhaps to marry. To marry my beloved Ogbotanga.

MYRTLE. That's such a clever name, Penny.

CLARENCE. (*Collapsing into his chair.*) I give up.

PENNY. In Balamubu it means "Smiling Giant." You see, Ogbo is nine feet tall. Tall and strong. Strong like me. We played catch with pigs.

MYRTLE. *(Howls with laughter.)* Oh Penny, you are the most entertaining person I've ever met.

(CLARENCE just stares at both of them, shaking his head despondently.)

PENNY. I am?

MYRTLE. You ought to be in a comedy club. Don't you think she ought to be in a comedy club, Clarence? Clarence?

CLARENCE. Go home, Penny.

PENNY. *(Caught off guard.)* Home?

CLARENCE. Don't come back until tomorrow morning. We'll discuss your status then.

PENNY. My "status"?

CLARENCE. Here at Graceland.

PENNY. You're not considering *firing* me, are you, Mr. Olander?

CLARENCE. I said we'll talk about it tomorrow.

PENNY. But I want to know *now.*

CLARENCE. I cannot discuss anything right now, Penny. I feel like somebody is unscrewing my head.

PENNY. *(Gets up and starts out the door.)* May I say how much I really like it here?

MYRTLE. *(Waits for Clarence to respond. When HE doesn't.)* And we like having you here, Penny.

(PENNY makes a weak attempt at a smile and walks slowly out of the room. MYRTLE waits until after SHE is gone before speaking to Clarence.)

MYRTLE. Before you make a decision on Penny, I want you to do one thing.
CLARENCE. *(Wearily.)* What?
MYRTLE. Talk to Vivian.
CLARENCE. Vivian? And just how am I supposed to do that? She's been dead for three years.
MYRTLE. I didn't say it was going to be a two-way conversation, Clarence. I just said talk to her. I think you know what I mean.

(LIGHTS fade out here and CROSS FADE up in the classroom. The room is painted with soft BLUE LIGHT. MS. DANLEY sits behind the desk. PENNY enters, and goes to stand beside her.)

MS. DANLEY. I asked you to stay after school, Penny, because I wanted to talk to you about *this*. *(SHE holds up a child's writing tablet.)* I can tell you gave the subject a lot of thought.
PENNY. Yes, ma'am.
MS. DANLEY. This kind of effort deserves an "A."

(PENNY brightens.)

MS. DANLEY. It *deserves* an "A," Penny—but it doesn't get one.

(PENNY's face drops.)

MS DANLEY. In fact, it doesn't even get a "D." Am I being cruel, Penny?

(PENNY nods.)

MS DANLEY. Well I'm sure there are those who would agree with you. But you know what? I don't give a rat's behind *what* those people think. Because this isn't *their* classroom, now is it? Is it?

PENNY. No, ma'am.

MS. DANLEY. It's mine. I am the queen and they aren't. Who is the queen, Penny?

PENNY. You are.

MS. DANLEY. And who are *they*?

PENNY. They are *not* the queen.

MS. DANLEY. Exactly right. Gold star for you. (*SHE opens one of the drawers to the desk and takes out a glittery, stick-on star. SHE presses it to Penny's forehead where it remains through the rest of the scene. SHE then hands PENNY the tablet.*) Read me your theme.

PENNY. I have to read it aloud?

MS. DANLEY. Yes, aloud.

PENNY. I get nervous reading aloud.

MS. DANLEY. Would you rather read it in front of Principal Furman?

PENNY. (*Shakes her head, then clears her throat. Reading from the tablet.*) "What I Want to Be When I Grow Up," by Penelope Anne Patterson. (*Clears her throat again.*) "What I want to be when I grow up is a teacher. I think teaching would be fun and especially if you like to be around children. You can go on field trips like the zoo and play Twister and go to museums with Mona Lisa and go to the zoo."

MS. DANLEY. (*Interrupting.*) You mentioned the zoo twice.

PENNY. I'm sorry.

MS. DANLEY. Go on.

PENNY. (*Reading.*) "Most of all I think I would be very nice to the children, most especially the children that have fathers and mothers who are not at home because they are dead. I would be very nice and not mean. I would be a good teacher I promise."

MS. DANLEY. Stop. Back up.

(PENNY takes a step back.)

MS. DANLEY. No, Penny. I mean back up in your composition. Go back to "I would be very nice and not mean." Now right after the word "mean" you've written something and scratched it out. It looks like three words. What are those three words, Penny?

PENNY. I don't remember.

MS. DANLEY. I think you *do* remember.

PENNY. I really don't.

MS. DANLEY. Well then, we'll just have to figure it out, won't we? Come over here.

PENNY. I don't want to.

MS. DANLEY. (*Losing patience.*) Come over here, Penny. Let us look at the three words together. (*MS. DANLEY grabs Penny's arm and pulls her to her.*)

PENNY. (*Struggling to wrench free.*) I have to get home.

MS. DANLEY. As if your foster parents cared *when* you got home. The first word, Penny. Let us decipher the first word. Is it "like"?

PENNY. Maybe.

MS. DANLEY. Maybe? Can you think of any other word it could be?

PENNY. No.

MS. DANLEY. "I would be very nice and not mean *like:*" Like who, Penny? Mean like who?

PENNY. Mr. Furman?

MS. DANLEY. That looks like "Miss," Penny. Miss who?

PENNY. You're hurting my arm!

MS. DANLEY. Miss who?

PENNY. My arm!

MS. DANLEY. (*Let's go.*) Look at your arm, Penny. Look at it.

(*PENNY looks at her arm.*)

MS. DANLEY. Is it bruised? Did I break the skin? Are you bleeding all over the floor? Answer me.

PENNY. (*Softly.*) No.

MS. DANLEY. No, what?

PENNY. No, ma'am. I'm not bleeding all over the floor.

MS. DANLEY. Have I ever hurt any of you children?

PENNY. (*Shakes her head.*) But you send us to Mr. Furman.

MS. DANLEY. Has Mr. Furman ever laid a finger on you?

PENNY. (*Shaking her head.*) No. But he makes us sit with the special education class. It's very scary in there.

MS. DANLEY. (*Mocking.*) "Very scary in there." Well, welcome to the real world, missy. The real world, I'm sorry to be the one to have to tell you, just happens to be a very scary place. But where is it written that it's *my* job, *my job*, Penny, to have to protect you from it? I am not paid to coddle you kids. I am paid to teach. And perhaps one of the first things a child should learn is how to grow up. Are you listening to me?

PENNY. (*Softly.*) Yes, ma'am.

MS. DANLEY. Then tell me once again who I am.

PENNY. You are the queen.

MS. DANLEY. And what would you like to be when *you* grow up, little Penny Patterson?

PENNY. (*Without conviction.*) I would like to be a queen too.

MS. DANLEY. Very good. Come here. (*SHE gets up.*) Come sit here on the throne.

(*Very slowly, almost cautiously, PENNY sits down behind the teacher's desk.*)

MS. DANLEY. You sit right there and work on your theme while I go down the hall for a few minutes.

PENNY. I really should get home.

MS. DANLEY. You weren't listening to me, princess. No one is waiting for you at home. No one is waiting because no one cares. You are unloved, Penny. You are an unloved little girl. Must I continually remind you of that fact?

(PENNY shakes her head.)

MS. DANLEY. You will make a wonderful queen. I'm sure of it.

(MS. DANLEY exits. PENNY peels the stick-on star from her forehead as the BLUE LIGHT is replaced by NATURAL LIGHTING. SHE sits for a moment staring pensively ahead. The reverie ends and SHE snaps back to the present. SHE finds herself once again in her Graceland classroom.)

PENNY. Now, where was I? Oh yes. *(SHE pulls out the portable tape player and sets it on the desk.)* I was about to tell you ...

(Sound of jungle MUSIC.)

PENNY. ... how I came to be called "Queen of the Congo." It is indeed a wonderful story!

*(The MUSIC swells as PENNY begins to tell her story. From this point on we will not be able to hear what SHE is saying although the excitement of her story will be easily conveyed to us through wild animated gestures and mime. It is also at this moment, down in the administrative offices that a brief shadow play will begin: simultaneously and with almost perfectly matched choreography, CLARENCE and MYRTLE both glance up from the work on their desks, and look about their respective rooms, trying, it seems, to define for themselves what it is they're hearing. THEY get up

*from their desks and cross to their windows. THEY
spend a moment or two here, and then meet in the
implied doorway which separates their offices.
RICHARD rushes in and joins the discussion. Back
upstairs PENNY continues her story, unaware that
DORIS is now gaping at her from the hallway. DORIS
remains for a moment, trying unsuccessfully to cover
her ears—SHE'S got several dozen pencils in her
hands—then storms off down the hallway toward
Clarence's office. SHE charges into the office, pencils
flying, and describes what she has just witnessed, then
leads CLARENCE, MYRTLE and RICHARD back up
to the hallway just outside of Penny's classroom where
the MUSIC now grows softer and we are able to hear
the conclusion of Penny's story.)*

PENNY.—but among all those Balamubu tribesmen I
could not find a single one who would believe me. "You
speak of newfound prowess ..." they laughed scornfully.
"... and yet just this morning you lay weak in bed with the
dreaded crocodile fever."
DORIS. (*To Clarence.*) Are you just going to let her
continue on like that?

(*But this seems to be exactly what Clarence intends to do
as HE and the OTHERS watch on with rapt
fascination.*)

PENNY. "Prove that this is not the fever talking," the
tribesmen said. "Prove that you do indeed possess the
power you say you do. That in his palsied hand the witch
doctor's magic healing rattle did somehow imbue you with

strength beyond measure. Prove this, She-rumba, you whom the village yakkety-yaks regard as too weak to even lift a tiny child from his sleeping mat."

RICHARD. I want to hunt wild game with this woman—are you listening to me, people?

(MYRTLE shhh's Richard.)

PENNY. "What, then, would be your challenge?" I asked. "To lift a child," they replied. "We challenge you to lift a single child into the air." I laughed. "I will do much better than that, my fellow tribesmen. I will lift every child in the village. Bring me first the orphaned ones. I shall place these highest on my shoulders. The finest view shall be theirs."

CLARENCE. *(To himself, lost in the story.)* Yes, do get the orphans first.

(HE catches himself, but it is too late; his COMPANIONS give him odd looks.)

PENNY. "Then bring me the others—I shall carry all the children in the village on my firm and sinewy shoulders." Which I proceeded to do—quite easily I might add. I even had strength left over to balance a young ewe-lamb on my head. And the tribesmen—should I say it?—were mightily impressed.

RICHARD. *(Having fun.)* As are we, Penny. As most certainly are we.

PENNY. Then seeing the kindly witch doctor hobbling with his bamboo walker out of his hut, I set all the little children down and began to dance. This was my way of paying him for his services. "What is the name of that dance?" the witch doctor asked. "I call it the Dance of the Twelve Pleasures," I answered. "And one of my biggest pleasures will be teaching it to my students as we embark on our own African adventure in the fall." So let's all get up from our desks—up, up, up! Join me, boys and girls, in the Dance of the Twelve Pleasures!

(The jungle MUSIC swells again, now accompanied by a strong, pulsating African DRUM BEAT. PENNY dances, stooped slightly, much of her movement from the waist, her arms fluttering in the air. RICHARD can't stand it any longer and bounds into the classroom.)

RICHARD. Teach *me*, you beautiful jungle goddess! Teach me *all* the pleasures!

(HE begins to dance with her, trying his best to emulate her moves in his own stiff, nerdy way. PENNY regards him curiously, somewhat suspiciously, but only for a moment. There is too much joy in the room ... and just outside the room; MYRTLE is waving at her and beginning to move with the music.)

MYRTLE. Did you feel that, Clarence?
CLARENCE. Feel what?
MYRTLE. The air conditioning! It just came back on.
CLARENCE. (*An odd smile.*) You know, I think you're right.
MYRTLE. I feel like dancing, Clarence. I feel like dancing with *you*!

CLARENCE. No, Myrtle. I can't—don't—
DORIS. Myrtle Dixon, you look like an absolute fool.
MYRTLE. (*Now pushing Clarence into the classroom.*)
Get wild with me, Clarence. Get crazy!

(*MYRTLE succeeds in getting CLARENCE into the
classroom. SHE then begins to manipulate his arms,
wriggling them in imitation of Penny and Richard.*)

CLARENCE. (*Grabbing his back.*) Stop, Myrtle! I'm
going to pull my back—

(*CLARENCE and MYRTLE are both stooped over now;
MYRTLE dancing, CLARENCE clutching his back in
pain. JULES RICHTER appears beside DORIS in the
hallway. HE is wearing a suit. CLARENCE sees him
first, then MYRTLE and PENNY. THEY freeze.
RICHARD continues to dance alone. MYRTLE nudges
him. HE stops dancing and shuts off the music.*)

JULES. (*The voice of God.*) You didn't mention *this* in
your phone call, Ms. Crumley.
CLARENCE. (*Pulls himself up erect. Stiffly.*) Hello,
Jules. (*To Doris, sarcastically.*) Thank you for informing
me of the Superintendent's little visit, Doris.
JULES. (*Takes a long look at Penny.*) Do I know you?
PENNY. I don't think so.
RICHARD. You must be confusing She-rumba here
with some other jungle monarch.
JULES. (*To Clarence, indicating Richard.*) What's this
marine doing here?

RICHARD. I *used* to be a marine, Superintendent General sir, but now I'm into a much more dangerous line of work.

JULES. (*To Clarence.*) This man is one of yours?

CLARENCE. (*Cowed.*) Yes.

JULES. (*Inspects Clarence and Myrtle.*) You two on the way to the beach?

CLARENCE. You know how hot it's been here the last few days, Jules.

JULES. It certainly doesn't feel that way *now*. Feels quite pleasant in fact.

MYRTLE. The air conditioning just came back on.

JULES. Just now? Just this very minute?

(*MYRTLE nods. JULES smiles suspiciously and turns to Doris; indicating Penny.*)

MYRTLE. Is this the teacher you were talking about?

DORIS. Yes. That's her. Penny Patterson.

JULES. I'd like to have a word with you in your office, Clarence.

CLARENCE. All right.

(*CLARENCE and JULES start out of the classroom. JULES stops beside Doris.*)

JULES. You have pencil smudges all over your ears, Ms. Crumley.

DORIS. (*Mortified.*) I *do*?

(*SHE begins to wipe furiously at her ears as JULES and CLARENCE walk on.*)

PENNY. (*To the class.*) Let's take our seats, children.

(*Something in the hall stops JULES dead in his tracks.*)

JULES. What the hell is *that* supposed to be?
CLARENCE. Elvis Presley.
JULES. That doesn't look anything like Elvis. It looks like a naked leper or something. It makes me want to puke.
CLARENCE. I'll have it taken down.
JULES. You do that.

(*HE moves briskly down the hallway. CLARENCE has to run to catch up with him.*)

DORIS. (*To Myrtle.*) Did I miss a spot?
MYRTLE. (*Worried, her mind obviously on Penny.*) What?
DORIS. The pencil smudges—are they all gone?
MYRTLE. (*Turns to Doris. With feigned sweetness.*) Oh no, honey. Now you look like you have big hairy sideburns. I really think you ought to go kill yourself.

(*DORIS is not amused. SHE hurries off, still pawing at her ears.*)

PENNY. Let's put our shoes on, children. (*To Richard.*) It's getting very cool in here, don't you think?
RICHARD. Yeager's probably testing the system.
PENNY. I don't want the children to get too chilled.
RICHARD. I'll go check on him.

(RICHARD exits. JULES and CLARENCE cross into Clarence's inner office. JULES stares at all the pencils on the floor. CLARENCE kicks a few out of Jules' path.)

CLARENCE. Would you like to sit down? Here, have a nut. (*HE offers the nut bowl to Jules.*)

JULES. (*Ignoring the offer.*) You want to tell me what the hell's going on around here, Clarence?

CLARENCE. Nothing's going on. Everything's under control.

JULES. Ms. Crumley doesn't think so. After what I just witnessed upstairs, I'm inclined to agree with her.

CLARENCE. Sometimes our teachers get a little over-enthused.

JULES. Are we talking about teaching, Clarence, or African fertility dances?

CLARENCE. I just meant—

JULES. What do you know about this woman, this Ms. Patterson?

CLARENCE. I know that the kids really seem to like her.

JULES. Has it not occurred to you at any point during the last three days that she might be a little bit *off?*

CLARENCE. I admit she's *different.*

JULES. *Different?* This is how you describe a woman who throws desks out of windows?

CLARENCE. (*Softly.*) They were very old desks.

JULES. What?

CLARENCE. Nothing.

JULES. Fire her, Clarence.

*(CLARENCE wants to say something but can't quite
come out with it.)*

JULES. Today.
CLARENCE. But—*(Stops.)*
JULES. But what?
CLARENCE. Maybe I could talk to her. Maybe I could
get her to—
JULES. *(Shaking his head.)* You can't talk to these
people. They're never going to get it. I've worked with
these non-conformist types before. It's not in their nature
to accept any kind of regimentation. They teach on a
whim. Sometimes the whim of the day is simply not to
teach at all.
MYRTLE. *(To Penny, hugging herself from the cold.)*
This place is getting downright frigid. *(SHE turns to go.)*
You'll be okay, honey?

(PENNY nods. MYRTLE exits.)

JULES. You know, I remember a situation much the
same as this—about six years ago when I was
superintendent down in Bluff City. One of the teachers, I
forget her name, she reports for work wearing this
ridiculous dress with dogs all over it. Spends the day
howling. Howling, Clarence.

*(CLARENCE has made the connection; JULES doesn't
detect.)*

CLARENCE. What did you—what did you do?
JULES. What do *you* think I did?

PENNY. (*Now pacing to keep warm. To her students.*) Why don't we get up and move around—get the blood circulating?

(*MYRTLE has now reached the outer office. CLARENCE hears her coming in.*)

CLARENCE. (*For Jules' benefit, last names only.*) Ms. Dixon?
MYRTLE. (*Entering inner office.*) Yes, Mr. Olander?
CLARENCE. What's with the air conditioning? It's freezing in here.
MYRTLE. I don't know. Richard is trying to find Mr. Yeager.
PENNY. (*To another student.*) Rub your arms and legs. Briskly. That's right. (*SHE is worried now, and not doing a good job of hiding this fact from her students.*) Maybe we should do some calisthenics.

(*SHE attempts a couple of jumping jacks, then stops. A memory has been triggered and materializes in limbo downstage: MS. DANLEY, lit by BLUE LIGHT, speaking to her unseen class. LIGHT fades out in Clarence's office.*)

MS. DANLEY. You will stop bouncing about and sit down this instant! (*Claps her hands together.*) I said to SIT DOWN! (*Her attention focused on one spot.*) Penny, are you deaf?
PENNY. (*Speaks to Ms Danley as if she were in the room with her.*) No, ma'am.
MS. DANLEY. Then why will you not do as I ask?

PENNY. I don't want to sit down, Miss Danley. My desk is cold.

MS. DANLEY. All of our desks are cold, Penny.

PENNY. When I can't move around, my feet start to hurt.

MS. DANLEY. You are not the only one in this room with frozen feet, Penny. Now you will take your seat just like the others and you will remain in that seat until Mr. Furman returns with further instructions. There are certain procedures which must be followed in emergencies such as these.

PENNY. I do not think I will wait, Miss Danley. I think I will go down the street to that old church on the corner where I know it will be warm.

MS. DANLEY. You will do nothing of the kind.

PENNY. (*To her fellow students.*) You must all come with me. You must gather all your stuff together and come with me to the church. Mr. Furman is very busy right now and he has probably forgotten about us.

MS. DANLEY. You will sit down—All of you! You will stay right where you—Do not, I repeat, *do not* go out that door—you, you come back here. You come back here this very instant!

(*MS. DANLEY watches helplessly as her class walks out on her. SHE remains illuminated, alone and defeated, as PENNY returns to the present.*)

PENNY. (*To her class.*) Who wants to go to the mall and learn about sales tax? (*Listens.*) Then let's do it!

(SHE begins to usher her students out of the room as LIGHTS fade out over both PENNY and MS. DANLEY and come up in Clarence's inner office. MYRTLE is wearing a windbreaker. SHE hands CLARENCE a sweater.)

CLARENCE. *(As HE takes it.)* You sure you don't want to wear it?

MYRTLE. No. This is fine.

CLARENCE. *(Putting on the sweater.)* Maybe you should try to find out what happened to Richard. *(SHE nods and goes out to her desk.)*

JULES. I've got to go, Clarence. I'm already late for an appointment with the mayor. You'll do that thing we talked about?

(Before Clarence can answer, MYRTLE's voice booms out over the public address microphone.)

MYRTLE. RICHARD? MYRTLE HERE. GIVE US A REPORT ON THE A.C. PROBLEM AS SOON AS YOU CAN.

JULES. What is this—a used car dealership? You and I are going to have a long talk about the way you've let things slide around here, Clarence.

(CLARENCE nods.)

JULES. If you will remember, I appointed you to this job because you said you were a Covington man. You weren't just saying what I wanted to hear, now were you?

CLARENCE. No. I *was* a Covington man.

JULES. "Was"? What are you now, Clarence?
CLARENCE. I don't know.
JULES. This disturbs me.
CLARENCE. I'm just being honest.
JULES. I appreciate your honesty, Clarence. I'm still disturbed. (*JULES now sees something out the window.*) What is that?
CLARENCE. That's a picture of Elvis getting a karate lesson.
JULES. I'm talking about outside. What's going on out there?

(*THEY both move closer to the window. CLARENCE now sees what Jules sees.*)

CLARENCE. I don't —Myrtle?

(*MYRTLE rushes in.*)

CLARENCE. Do you know what she's doing?
MYRTLE.It looks like she's taking them for a walk.
JULES. A *walk*?
MYRTLE. It makes perfect sense. It's far too cold in here for those light summer clothes they're all wearing.
JULES. May I ask who gave her permission to do this?
CLARENCE. I suppose she gave herself permission.
JULES. Do I take it that Graceland is simply riding along on auto pilot these days, Clarence? (*HE doesn't give Clarence a chance to answer and turns to Myrtle.*) You will stop Ms. Patterson from leaving the school grounds. You will bring her back to this office immediately.

MYRTLE. I'll send the kids over to the playground, Clarence.
CLARENCE. All right.

(MYRTLE goes out as RICHARD comes in.)

RICHARD. Clarence?

(CLARENCE and JULES turn to face Richard.)

RICHARD. We got a problem.
CLARENCE. What's wrong?
RICHARD. Yeager's bombed out of his gourd. I found him down in the boiler room singing "Winter Wonderland" and describing how he was going to make it start snowing out of the sprinkler system.
CLARENCE. I knew something like this was going to happen. Is he still down there?
RICHARD. Yeah. But you can't talk to him. He's going to be out of it for a while.

(RICHARD massages his fist. CLARENCE frowns.)

RICHARD. I didn't know what else to do, Clarence. He was very uncooperative.
CLARENCE. So, what's the situation with the air conditioning?
RICHARD. Not good. It doesn't look like we're going to be able to shut the thing off without losing power to the whole building. I'm going to take my kids outside. I think you ought to get the rest of the teaching staff to do the same.

JULES. Wait a minute. You want to evacuate the whole school because the damn thermostat's dropped a couple of degrees?

RICHARD. Begging your pardon, Superintendent General *sir*, there *is* no thermostat. I think Yeager hid it somewhere.

JULES. I'm not going to permit this.

CLARENCE. I don't think we have a choice.

JULES. The hell we don't. Everyone stays put while I place an emergency phone call to L, G and W.

CLARENCE. That could still take time. (*To Richard.*) Take the children outside.

JULES. Are you countermanding me here, Clarence?

DORIS. (*Enters. Before Clarence can answer.*) My room is like a meat locker. I cannot administer the PTQSTAT inside a meat locker!

RICHARD. We're taking all the kids outside, Doris.

JULES. No one is doing anything until this situation has been evaluated by someone from Light, Gas and Water. I advise you both to return to your classrooms until further notice.

(*DORIS and RICHARD turn to Clarence. The time has come for Clarence to say what will probably be the most important thing he's ever said in his life. HE takes a deep breath.*)

CLARENCE. Clear the school. This man is a dickhead.

RICHARD. (*Grinning.*) You got it, sir.

(*DORIS finds it hard not to smile. SHE and RICHARD exit. JULES takes his time before speaking. Finally:*)

JULES. You're fired, Clarence.
CLARENCE. Why am I not surprised?
JULES. You know, you really had me fooled.
CLARENCE. Maybe I had myself fooled. Sure you won't have a nut, Jules?

(HE makes to offer the bowl of pistachios to Jules, then tosses them all into the air just as MYRTLE and PENNY enter. MYRTLE stares at Clarence incredulously.)

MYRTLE. Are you all right?
CLARENCE. (*Grinning broadly.*) I'm fine. (*Beat.*) I'm also unemployed.
PENNY. Please don't tell me this is all because of me.
CLARENCE. It is and it isn't. Doesn't matter. Doesn't matter one damn bit.
MYRTLE. Penny, honey, you look very cold in that outfit. Maybe you should put something on over it. Didn't I see your dog dress hanging in the closet down in the teacher's lounge?

(As PENNY nods, this fact registers with JULES like a slap in the face.)

JULES. (*To Penny.*) I knew I had seen you somewhere before.
PENNY. (*To Myrtle.*) Mr. Richter used to be the superintendent of the Bluff City School System. I taught there for about three weeks.

JULES. (*Coldly.*) You must be a real pro at this by now.

PENNY. Not really. This is the first time I've ever won.

JULES. You call this winning? I just terminated your employment here.

PENNY. (*Not upset, just curious, to Clarence.*) He did?

(CLARENCE nods.)

MYRTLE. (*To Jules.*) Am I fired too?

JULES. This isn't a spree, Ms. Dixon.

MYRTLE. Well, you certainly wouldn't expect me to keep working here without Clarence and Penny. (*A beat.*) I quit! (*To Clarence.*) Now we'll *have* to start up that little private school, won't we?

CLARENCE. (*Smiling thoughtfully.*) I suppose we will, Myrtle.

MYRTLE. And Penny—you'll teach at our school too, won't you, honey?

PENNY. I'd love to.

MYRTLE. (*To Clarence.*) You know who else we could get? That sweet Miss Poindexter who teaches at Riverview. She hasn't been too happy over there since Mr. Donald made her give up her hand puppets.

CLARENCE. Donald said she couldn't use the puppets?

MYRTLE. Not a single one.

PENNY. Mr. Richter used to teach with hand puppets. (*Now commanding the attention of everyone in the room.*) Back when he was a teacher—in Bluff City. He used them all the time. Didn't you, Mr. Richter?

JULES. I don't know what this woman is talking about.

PENNY. (*Confidentially, to Myrtle.*) Sewed all the little paisley outfits for them himself.

(*MYRTLE wants to laugh but tries hard to suppress it.*)

JULES. (*Almost like a child, to Clarence.*) This woman is lying! (*To Penny.*) You have no proof of this!

PENNY. (*Still to Myrtle.*) The teachers at Bluff City Elementary, they're still talking about it. The way he used to dance those little puppets all around his desk.

JULES. (*To Clarence.*) I'm not going to listen to any more of this.

CLARENCE. Your veins are bulging, Jules.

JULES. (*Still to Clarence.*) Can we talk in private?

CLARENCE. Not if it has anything to do with Penny.

JULES. (*Sotto voce.*) But Clarence, look at her. Isn't it obvious the woman is—you know—

CLARENCE. "Minus some buttons"?

JULES. Right.

CLARENCE. Of course it's obvious ...

(*MYRTLE reacts with surprise.*)

CLARENCE. On the other hand, forcing kids to freeze their asses off while you play the bumbling bureaucrat, that would be the product of sane and rational thought?

JULES. (*Has no defense. After a moment's rumination.*) All right. Nobody's fired. Everybody stays. We'll discuss the conditions later.

CLARENCE. No *conditions*, Jules. I won't work here if I've got to have you breathing down my neck every day.

JULES. We will talk about this later, Clarence. I am *very* late.

(HE starts out of the office and plows into RICHARD who has just entered and will not permit him to pass.)

JULES. You want to step aside, marine? I'm in a hurry here.

RICHARD. *(Having fun.)* Is that your BMW out in the parking lot? Looks like somebody let the air out of your tires.

JULES. *(Crosses quickly to the window. Fuming.)* I need to use a phone.

MYRTLE. *(To Jules, guarding the phone on her desk.)* There's a telephone down in the teacher's lounge, honey. You'll like it there—the wallpaper's all in paisley.

(JULES grunts and hurries out of the office. RICHARD gives him a mock salute as HE passes. MYRTLE hugs Clarence.)

CLARENCE. I'm so proud of you. I know Vivian would be too.

RICHARD. Sounds like some sort of celebration is in order here. *(To Penny.)* How about tonight? You. Me. My place. Don't change.

PENNY. *(Gently.)* Thank you but maybe some other night. I'm very tired.

*(SHE squeezes his hand; HE smiles, starts to exit. DORIS
    enters.)*

RICHARD. (*To Doris.*) Did you see Richter's car?

(SHE nods, a strange look on her face.)

RICHARD. Who do you think the culprit was—one of
yours or one of mine?
DORIS. (*Mischievously.*) Oh I don't think it was one
of the children.
MYRTLE. (*Shock.*) Why, Doris Crumley!
DORIS. He made fun of my face. Nobody touches me
and *nobody* makes fun of my face.
RICHARD. Gotta admit—it's a nice face ... (*Beat.*) ...
When you smile.

*(SHE beams like a lighthouse as HE escorts her out of the
    office.)*

PENNY. (*Taking CLARENCE'S hand.*) Thank you,
Mr. Olander.
CLARENCE. (*Correcting her.*) Clarence. (*HE smiles.*)
PENNY. I'll check on the children. (*SHE goes out. The
PHONE rings.*)
MYRTLE. This may be Ms. Pittman, Clarence. She
phoned earlier to ask if you still wanted her to come by on
Friday.
CLARENCE. I've changed my mind, Myrtle. I've
decided to keep all the Elvis stuff.
MYRTLE. Good for you! (*SHE picks up the phone.*)
Graceland Elementary School.

CLARENCE. I'm even thinking of doubling the collection.

MYRTLE. (*Into phone.*) One moment, Mr. Covington. (*To Clarence, her hand over the mouthpiece.*) Old R.J.'s returning your call, Clarence. (*Holds the phone out for him.*)

CLARENCE. Tell him I'm not in.

MYRTLE. (*Happily.*) He's not in, Mr. Covington. I don't know when he'll be back. Have a nice day.

(*SHE hangs up. CLARENCE and MYRTLE embrace. LIGHTS fade out here as BLUE LIGHT comes up in the class room. MS. DANLEY is sitting at her desk. PENNY walks through the shadows to join her.*)

PENNY. Miss Danley, the children are all safe and sound inside the church. There's a lady there who's making us all hot chocolate.

MS. DANLEY. You trudged all the way back over here to tell me that?

PENNY. Yes, ma'am. I thought you'd be worried.

MS. DANLEY. Thank you for letting me know, Penny.

PENNY. You're welcome. (*Beat.*) Would you like to join us?

MS. DANLEY. No, Penny. I think I'll stay here.

PENNY. All right. (*PENNY starts out.*)

MS. DANLEY. Penny?

PENNY. Yes?

MS. DANLEY. You don't think I'm a very good teacher, do you?

PENNY. No.

MS. DANLEY. Why is that?
PENNY. It's very cold in here, Miss Danley. I have to go.

(PENNY exits, leaving Ms. DANLEY alone at the desk. As LIGHTS slowly fade out we hear "The King" singing "Are You Lonesome Tonight.")

End of Play

COSTUME PLOT

CLARENCE OLANDER

<u>Day One</u>: white long-sleeved shirt, burgundy tie, grey slacks, navy suit coat, black shoes

<u>Day Two</u>: white long-sleeved shirt, grey slacks, light blue tie

<u>Day Three</u>: white short-sleeved shirt, beige dress pants, brown shoes, brown tie

<u>Day Four</u>: white short-sleeved shirt, navy tie, loud Bermuda shorts (red Hawaiian), black socks, black shoes; ADD sweater (from off)

MYRTLE DIXON

<u>Day One</u>: flowery summer blouse, off-white shorts, high-heeled sandals

<u>Day Two</u>: long-sleeved white shirt—rolled up sleeves, unbuttoned and tied at waist, olive green shorts, high-heeled sandals

<u>Day Three</u>: off-white shorts, green print short-sleeved blouse, high-heeled sandals

<u>Day Four</u>: khaki shorts, yellow short-sleeved blouse, white t-shirt, high-heeled sandals; ADD windbreaker (from off)

PENNY PATTERSON

<u>Day One</u>: short-sleeved white blouse, navy A-line skirt, flat black shoes, shoulder bag

<u>Day Two</u>: beige cotton summer dress, brown flat shoes, apron

<u>Day Three</u>: white summer dress with furry dog appliques and dog paw prints, flat brown shoes

<u>Day Four</u>: leopard skin jacket with fur sleeves, golden yellow balloon pants, black body leotard, patterned scarf worn around waist, flat brown shoes, crown of animal bones

MS. DANLEY

<u>Day One</u>: off-white laced (polyester) shirt dress, matching low-heeled pumps

<u>Day Two</u>: same as Day One

<u>Day Four</u>: same as Day One

RICHARD WINGFIELD

<u>Day Two</u>: khaki pants, white long-sleeved shirt, camouflage-patterned tie, penny loafers

<u>Day Four</u>: USMC t-shirt, camouflage-patterned fatigue pants, sneakers

DORIS CRUMLEY

<u>Day Two</u>: white long-sleeved blouse, plaid school girl skirt, white bobby socks, flat black saddle shoes

<u>Day Three</u>: short-sleeved white blouse, grey skirt, black saddle shoes

<u>Day Four</u>: short-sleeved pale orchid blouse, purple A-line skirt, black saddle shoes

JULES RICHTER

<u>Day Four</u>: charcoal grey business suit, white long-sleeved shirt, red "power tie," black shoes

PROPERTY PLOT

ACT I, DAY ONE

<u>Office presets</u>: telephone, bust of Elvis Presley, piles of paperwork, bowl of pistachio nuts (Clarence's desk); telephone, public address microphone, paperback novel, desktop thermometer, stack trays (Myrtle's desk)

<u>From off</u>: 3 cans of soda

<u>From Penny's bag</u>: apple, pineapple

ACT I, DAY TWO

<u>Office presets</u>: same as Day One

<u>From off</u>: 2 cans of soda

<u>Doris's personal properties</u>: clipboard and ruler

<u>Classroom presets</u>: chalk and eraser, empty egg carton

ACT I, DAY THREE

<u>Office presets</u>: same as Day One

<u>Doris's personal properties</u>: clipboard and ruler

ACT II, DAY FOUR

<u>Classroom presets</u>: chalk and eraser, portable tape recorder, child's writing tablet (from inside desk), supply of stick-on stars

<u>Office presets</u>: same as Day One

<u>From off</u>: bottle of aspirin, glass of water

<u>Doris's personal properties</u>: 20 - 30 pencils

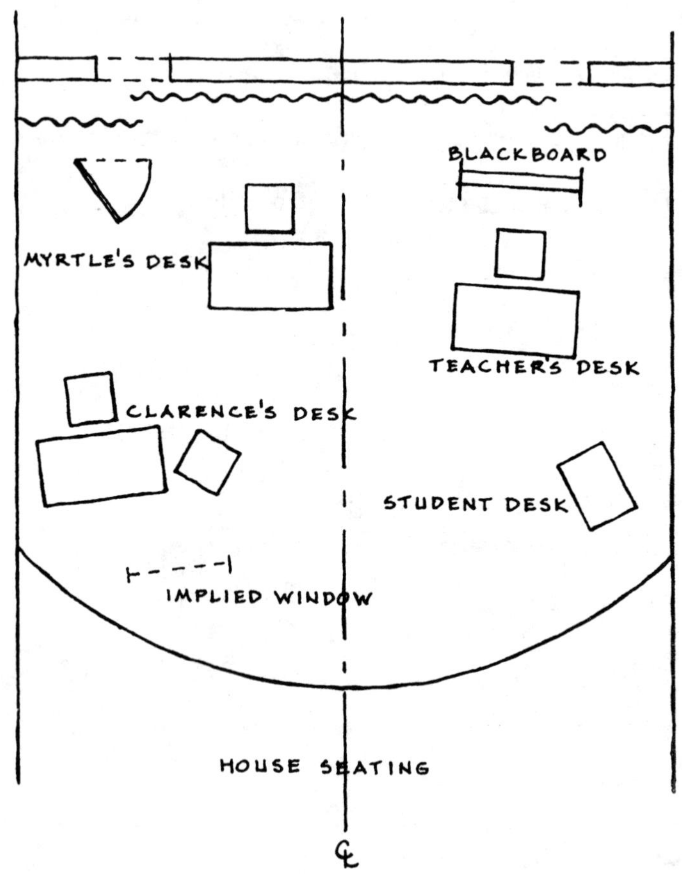

BACKSTAGE
BLACKBOARD
MYRTLE'S DESK
TEACHER'S DESK
CLARENCE'S DESK
STUDENT DESK
IMPLIED WINDOW
HOUSE SEATING

Other Publications for Your Interest

CINDERELLA WALTZ
(ALL GROUPS—COMEDY)
By DON NIGRO

4 men, 5 women—1 set

Rosey Snow is trapped in a fairy tale world that is by turns funny and a little frightening, with her stepsisters Goneril and Regan, her demented stepmother, her lecherous father, a bewildered Prince, a fairy godmother who sings salty old sailor songs, a troll and a possibly homicidal village idiot. A play which investigates the archetypal origins of the world's most popular fairy tale and the tension between the more familiar and charming Perrault version and the darker, more ancient and disturbing tale recorded by the brothers Grimm. Grotesque farce and romantic fantasy blend in a fairy tale for adults.

(#5208)

ROBIN HOOD
(LITTLE THEATRE—COMEDY)
By DON NIGRO

14 men, 8 women—(more if desired.) Unit set.

In a land where the rich get richer, the poor are starving, and Prince John wants to cut down Sherwood Forest to put up an arms manufactory, a slaughterhouse and a tennis court for the well to do, this bawdy epic unites elements of wild farce and ancient popular mythologies with an environmentalist assault on the arrogance of wealth and power in the face of poverty and hunger. Amid feeble and insane jesters, a demonic snake oil salesman, a corrupt and lascivious court, a singer of eerie ballads, a gluttonous lusty friar and a world of vivid and grotesque characters out of a Brueghel painting, Maid Marian loses her clothes and her illusions among the poor and Robin tries to avoid murder and elude the Dark Monk of the Wood who is Death and also perhaps something more.

(#20075)

Other Publications for Your Interest

THE VOICE OF THE PRAIRIE
(LITTLE THEATRE—COMIC/DRAMA)
By JOHN OLIVE

2 men, 1 women—to play a variety of roles
May be done with up to 10 actors—Unit Setting

When this play begins, we are listening to an old hobo (named "Poppy" by his avid companion young Davey Quinn) tell a tall tale. It is the early 1890's, and itinerant story tellers such as Poppy really were the voices of the prairie. Many years later, when Davey is grown up, he is "discovered" by radio entrepreneur Leon Schwab, telling his tales of Poppy and of Frankie the Blind Girl, whom he rescued from a cruel father and with whom he went on a cross-country adventure. Schwab thinks Quinn's stories would attract an audience for radio, the "wave of the future". Sure enough, David Quinn becomes famous as the Voice of the Prairie, as the cleverly-constructed play cross-cuts between scenes of Leon and David and scenes of young Davey and Frankie the Blind Girl, on the lam, in search of adventure. These scenes culminate in the unfortunate separation of Davey and Frankie, as Frankie is recognized, captured and sent back home. David Quinn, the grown-up Voice of the Prairie, has not seen or heard from her since; until, that is, Leon locates her in hopes of using his discovery of the actual, famous Frankie the Blind Girl for its sentimental value, to keep the new F.C.C. off his back. Will David forgive Frankie for leaving him so many years ago? Will Frankie agree to help Leon avoid jail for broadcasting without a license? "Endearing."—N.Y. Times. "That rare thing: a small, skillful play with a deft heart."—Los Angeles Times. "Beguiling entertainment and as American as corn."—Hartford Advocate. "First-rate entertainment. I can't remember when I last so enjoyed a play."—Torrington Register Citizen. Slightly Restricted.

(#24047)

CARELESS LOVE
(LITTLE THEATRE—DRAMA)
By JOHN OLIVE

1 male, 1 woman—Unit set

What a terrific little play for an actress and actor to sink their teeth into! And, it's about something that matters: committment, and responsibility, in love. When we first meet Jack, he is an aspiring actor, serious about his career but not very serious about his girl-friend, Martha, a waitress who is an aspiring dancer, who is a lot more serious about Jack. The couple drifts along on a cloud of good times — until Martha gets pregnant, at which time a *Choice* must be made. As the debate over their options progresses, Jack's acting career starts to take off; and, he starts to think more seriously about his life and his responsibilities. Unfortunately, at the same time Martha has been driven into self-absorption by Jack's carelessness, and has made a decision which is right for her, she thinks: she has decided to give the child up for adoption. So — at just about the time Jack is ready to make an emotional committment to Martha and to their child, it is too late: Martha has had the baby and put it up for adoption. This was, after all, *her* decision to make. Right? In the end, Martha is a self-sufficient contemporary woman, who makes her own choices. It is Jack who will hurt forever, from the pain of eternal separation from his child. "Bittersweet." — Variety. "In the delicacy of its writing, in the truth of its details...it is a most lovely, most satisfying evening in the theatre."—Chicago Tribune. "A lovely little play...works a winsome magic."—Philadelphia Daily News.

(#5237)